World Schooling
How to Revolutionize
Your Child's Education
Through Travel

ISBN: 9781520958507

Table of Contents

Foreword

The strict 'sit still' all day regime that my first school experience provided wasn't great. It didn't provide room for playing or satisfy my desire to explore. Boredom struck fast, I had incapable teachers and eventually even refused to go to school.

When my parents transferred me to a school based on the principles of Rudolf Steiner, my world changed, partly because of the school's philosophy, but mainly because I was very fortunate to meet an incredible and open-minded teacher who valued more than just preparing his students for tests.

Our class often had field trips that connected us to the real world. We would help a local farmer when we discussed farming or visit a museum when we learned about Cleopatra and Tutankhamun. After studying the ancient Egyptian hieroglyphs from a textbook, it was extremely rewarding to put that theory into practice and recognize those same hieroglyphs on real ancient stone engravings.

Conversely, as a child, my wife Brenda did not travel further than the next city from where she lived with her parents, brother and sister. Her first flight came when she was already 17 years old, which she paid for with her own money, earned by working on a local farm. Her family was afraid to go further afield because it was 'the unknown' and they were convinced that they did not have enough money to explore the great wide world.

When school holidays were over, it was a tradition in her school for the teacher to conduct a group conversation with the class about where all the children had spent the school holiday. Each child told their story and Brenda was always one of the few that had simply stayed at home. She felt sadness because she knew that she was missing something – she could not share her experiences in discovering the 'big' world because she had none.

As she grew up, she gained an increasing desire to explore new grounds and stretch her comfort zone. She wanted to change and do things completely different with her daughter than what her parents had done. She knew that it would never be the right time to travel – that there would always be some reason to stay at home. There would always be a convenient excuse as to why today just isn't the right day. Something would come up and plans would be put off until tomorrow when the magical "right time" came along.

As a couple, we realized that life is short, the world is wide and you only have one chance to make this one count. If we truly wanted to travel, if we truly wanted to live our dreams, we had to find a way to make it happen, now.

And that's what we did.

There were some difficult, life-changing events that led to the major decision to quit our 9-to-5 jobs, sell our house, two cars and all our stuff, and travel the world. I had a total burnout in 2008, Brenda's father was diagnosed with cancer, and soon after that Brenda's best friend (only 28 years old at the time) died from cancer in 2015. These events changed what we valued in life significantly. Long workdays away from our daughter and waiting until retirement to travel and enjoy life (when you have bad knees, weak lungs or may not even be alive anymore) didn't sound like a great value proposition.

The passing of time and the arrival of location independent work enabled our family to move around the world affordably while spending more time together. We embraced a minimalistic mindset and are now traveling full time with only two seven kilogram (14.5 pounds) backpacks. During our journey, we have met dozens of families running into the same challenges. This inspired us to found Nomad Family, a global community committed to empowering all traveling families to really connect and achieve their ambitions.

One of the challenges these families face is education. How do we prepare our children for a future in this rapidly globalizing world? How do we teach them skills like complex problem solving, critical thinking and creativity? How can we stimulate their emotional intelligence? What do we want to teach our children? How can we give them what they need to live, learn and work?

There is simply no magical one-size-fits-all answer. Education is a very personal thing, especially since most parents want to have 'the best' for their child, and 'the best' is very subjective. However, to a certain degree, our children can only succeed if we risk failure in our quest for 'the best'. Overcoming and learning from failure is key in one's development. That doesn't give us a carte blanche to simply set out to fail, but it does give us the freedom to look for something better than what we already have. For our family, this endeavor to give our daughter 'the best' includes world schooling.

World schooling is both learning from the world, as well as the parent's active engagement in it. Parents have to facilitate education, as well as encourage and support their children along the way. The world is an amazing place that has a lot to offer.

Imagine the impact on a child's education when they learn things in their authentic context. Reading hieroglyphs, not from a textbook, but in a real tomb in Egypt. Learning a foreign language, not from an audio recording, but by playing with children that natively speak that language. That is exactly what world schooling offers: the ability to combine learning from theory with practical elements in a local setting. It enriches you as a person, gradually developing a genuine understanding of the world around us.

Ashley has not only written an inspiring book for those who want to have an active role in their child's education, she has also provided different perspectives on education and the answers to the Whys, Whats and How To's of education through travel – all of this backed by research from leading experts in education, childhood development, and educational technology. You'll find everything you need to know to start your own educational journey.

In the end, we are responsible for our children's development. We want to prepare our children for the future as adequately as we can. As Dr. Stephen Covey said: "Begin with the end in mind." So what do you want your kids to have learned in the end?

Let's start making the world our classroom.

Gawin and Brenda Brave
Las Palmas de Gran Canaria, 2017

Introduction

"Travel is fatal to prejudice, bigotry, and narrow-mindedness, and
many of our people need it sorely on these accounts. Broad,
wholesome, charitable views of men and things cannot be acquired by
vegetating in one little corner of the earth all one's lifetime."
Mark Twain - Innocents Abroad

The moment had arrived: high school graduation. And there I was, sitting up on the stand with my fellow valedictorians. My graduating class had somehow produced twenty valedictorians that year and so the school came up with a clever way to involve more of us with a group speech. While there was still a speech from the smartest valedictorian of us all, our little group got the privilege of sitting on the stand and imparting some final words of wisdom to our fellow graduates.

It was an honor, for sure. However, that experience changed the way I saw education forever.

After our speech was over and the commencement was in full swing, I began to observe each and every one of my fellow graduates as they approached the stage and accepted their diploma folders. While I went to a rather large school, I knew almost every one of my 400+ classmates and had made a significant effort to at least know each of their names. As they passed, I couldn't resist the opportunity to reflect on the incredible futures they each had ahead of them.

And then this peculiar thought exploded onto the scene of my adolescent observations: "I may be on the stand," I thought, "and I may have won 'the game' of high school by coming out on top with a 4.0, but I'm pretty sure that many of the students who aren't sharing this stand with me will end up being more successful, financially secure, and able to contribute to the world than I ever will."

I had won the game, so why did I feel like I had lost – or at least failed to gain – something important?

I had spent years perfecting my ability to perform inside an isolated, man-made construct known as the formal education system, and the system was now rewarding me warmly. Good grades, insane amounts of participation in extracurricular activities across diverse disciplines, and lovely little test scores had gotten me generous scholarships (and my place on the stand that night), but I couldn't shake the feeling that I was the one with the short end of the stick.

What was it that I had failed to gain? The answer came quickly: Connection to something REAL.

In that moment I realized that my head was full of ideas and concepts that would only fully serve me if I continued on the path of formal education. I had absolutely NO idea how I would use them in the "real world." And who knew if my college education would leave me in the same position!

What if, after years of university classes and expenses, I was no better off in terms of making a living or doing something of value in the world than my current predicament? What if college was just another arena for an overachieving student to be rewarded by the artificial system that had produced me?

The thought filled me with a little bit of fear, but it also produced a lot of curiosity and a touch of excitement. The fear was minimal because I recognized that I really had learned a lot during my K-12 years. The curiosity came as I began to recognize that grades didn't reflect someone's full ability and potential. And the excitement began to seep in because I finally realized that I was the one in control of changing my educational future.

That night, I decided I would do everything within my power to ensure that the rest of my experience with formal education would give me as much practical, real world knowledge and experience as the system would allow. I was going to use the system to serve my ends and wouldn't just content myself with A's and gold stars. I wanted an education that enabled me to actually do something REAL beyond the walls of a classroom.

And, for the most part, I was able to do just that. During my college years I traveled, had real world internships and participated in various research projects both on campus and abroad. I made sure to use every personalized class assignment to serve my ends and interests. Everything was an opportunity to get me just a little closer to the answers, practical knowledge and experience that I knew I would need once I donned that final cap and gown.

Many of those experiences (and one research project in particular) brought me to Mexico, where I met my husband and where we now live with our little boy. It has been a non-stop adventure. While we are not perpetual travelers, the challenges and opportunities of simply living in another country have filled my life with new experiences I never would have had otherwise. And I love it!

My greatest adventure of all, however, has been that of becoming a mother. And, as the circular nature of life would have it, my little boy has brought me back to the question of education.

At first, my questions were about whether we should enroll him (and any other siblings who may follow) in a private school versus a public one here in Mexico. When I wasn't too convinced by either of those options, I began to consider homeschooling. Then, my husband mentioned the idea of going back to the US and we began to look at bilingual schools – both private and public. But when the thought of living in the US for the rest of my life made me feel like I was suffocating, I knew that couldn't be the whole answer either.

Don't get me wrong, I love the United States. I really do. For starters, my family is there and I love them more than words can describe. I also love the heritage and principles upon which the United States was founded and – despite its flaws – have hope for its future. But I also really like the rest of the world! It is just a little too fascinating to leave it alone for long.

I also have this restless drive for adventure and a burning desire to do something to improve the general state of human existence on our planet. So, when I return to the overabundance and comforts of the US after living or traveling abroad, I tend to start singing along with Belle from Beurty and the Beast[1], *I want much more than this provincial life. I want adventure in the great wide somewhere! I want it more than I can tell.* (I know, it is a little cheesy, but it pretty much sums up my feelings!)

When I realized that the idea of living in the US for the entire period of our children's education wasn't that appealing to me, my questions began to take on a different form. Now, I asked, could I really enjoy adventure in "the great wide somewhere" and not jeopardize my son's education? Could I have "much more than a provincial life" and ensure that my children's future wasn't just promising, but the best I could give them?

Amidst all these questions, my globetrotting boss introduced me to a concept that I had never heard of before: world schooling. One peek at the idea and I was hooked. At its core, world schooling is the intersection of travel, family, adventure and learning, resulting in a truly hands-on, real-world education. As I began to uncover the ways and workings of world schoolers, it was as if I was seeing the possibilities for the first time – the endless possibilities – for the kind of education I could give my children.

And thus began the research: scouring the internet, eating up books, interviewing the people who were out there actually world schooling, reflecting on my years of educational research in college, drawing from my various teaching experiences in the recent past and discussing every little exciting discovery along the way with my husband, family and friends.

The more I learned, the more excited I got. The more I researched, the more I could see the possibilities. And (since writing has always been my way to think through new ideas), the more I dove into the topic of world schooling, the more I needed to write about it. And so I did! And, of course, the result is this book.

Now, being relatively new to the scene, I feel you and I probably share a lot of the same questions and concerns. What exactly is world schooling? Why is it a good idea? Why should I choose world schooling over some other form of education? How does world schooling work? How can I sustain a travel lifestyle, especially with kids? What resources are available for world schoolers? And on and on and on. I promise you that the answers to these questions and more are waiting in the pages to come.

More importantly, since my little boy had barely learned to say "mama" when I began researching this book, I have yet to implement any one strategy. Because of that, you have the fortune of meeting an author without an agenda. I'm not going to push one particular world schooling method on you over another, simply because I am still taking a look at them all myself. I have aimed to make this book the best aggregation of information and experiences on the subject to give you access to in-depth research on a plethora of ideas and approaches, all in one spot.

We'll look into the research of some of the leading experts in education, childhood development and educational technology; talk to families who have been successfully world schooling for years; get financial tips from fearless international travelers; and dissect every aspect of this world schooling thing so that by the end of this book you'll be ready to design your own educational adventure, pack your bags and head out into the world with your family right by your side.

Ready? Let's go!

Section One:
"Schooling"

Chapter One: The End Goal
What Is the Purpose of Education?

Adventure. Anticipation. Exciting. Challenging. Intense. Rewarding. Learning. Connections. Exhausting. Optimism. Travel. Liberation. Mind-expanding. Life changing. Curiosity. Family. Epic. Freedom. Happiness. Choices. Life. Opportunity. Education. Joy. Fun. Transformative. Thrilling. Intentional. Revolutionary.

All these words and more have been used to describe world schooling. But what exactly is it?

In its simplest form, world schooling is the combination of education and travel. But to leave it at that would do this revolutionary new approach to life and education a terrible injustice. In the introduction, I claimed that world schooling is the intersection of travel, family, adventure and learning. And it is. But it is so much more!

The challenge is that world schooling doesn't fit neatly into one concise definition. There are many ways to be a worldschooler (more on that in Section Two) and many ways to apply the principles of world schooling to your own family. There are even diverse ways to make a world schooling lifestyle educationally and financially possible (and we'll get to that in Section Three). Every family that chooses to world school will find their own approach.

What worldschoolers *do* have in common, however, is their unique mindset in regards to life and education.

The world schooling community grows on a daily basis as parents begin to question the essential nature of their 9-to-5 jobs and look for ways to lead a more fulfilling, adventurous life. While many are held back by the belief that family and extensive world travel do not mix, the newest additions to the world schooling community are those people who recognize the intrinsic educational value of travel. For these families, world travel is not an irresponsible quest for thrill seekers, but a responsible and intentional effort to provide their children with an incredible opportunity to learn from the world. The adventure is just the cherry on the top.

For worldschoolers around the globe, travel is a means of education. The world is their classroom. This, of course, is a very unconventional approach to life and learning that tends to illicit questions from friends, family and even strangers. Perhaps you're even asking some of those questions yourself. How can you ensure that a child really learns what they need to learn without a school or a place to call home?

All of these concerns beg the question: *What is the real purpose of education?* If we do not already know the answer to that question, it is difficult to know whether the kind of education we provide our children will successfully help them achieve its purpose. Once we know the purpose, however, it can be incredibly liberating to realize just how many options we have to achieving those ends. For worldschoolers in particular, how can we know that world schooling is an effective form of education until we know to what end such education is meant to be used?

While on the philosophical side of things, forming your personal vision of the purpose of education is a very important first step toward your world schooling journey that should not be ignored. Indeed, it shouldn't be ignored under any set of circumstances.

If you have already done your research, the next couple of chapters may be more of a review for you. If so, feel free to skim or skip ahead. However, if you are new to the alternative education scene and need a little help letting go of the belief that formal education is the only way to ensure your child's future success, read on.

Answering the Question

Think about it, why do we send our kids to school long hours every day, five days a week? What do we hope they will get out of the experience? Knowledge? Experience? Creativity? Character? Social skills? Job preparation? The reality is that they're probably getting a little bit of all those things – I know I did – but is it the ideal way to achieve those ends?

And how will we know if they've achieved the ultimate end goal if we haven't even defined it?

In one of his incredible TedTalks, the best-selling author Seth Godin put it this way: "What is school for? I don't think we're answering that question. I don't even think we're *asking* that question. Everyone seems to think they know what school is for, but we're not going to make anything happen until we can all agree about how we got here and where we're going."[2]

There is a lot to that quote, so let's break it down bit by bit. First off, most people aren't even asking the question about the purpose of education or, more specifically, school. Most people send their kids off to school each day because that is what they did, that is what everyone else is doing, and that is society's clean-cut path to a child's future.

I am not saying that is a bad thing. I am a strong believer in the importance of education and believe that every child in the world not only deserves a quality education, but also that the world needs every child to be educated. What I *am* saying is that just because we know the system is doing some good, we shouldn't be afraid to ask why it exists in the first place and what can be done to make it better.

The next point Seth Godin makes is that everyone thinks they know what school is for. And I would add that what everyone thinks varies greatly from person to person. The educational non-profit ASCD puts it this way: "If you were to ask even a relatively small group of teachers, administrators, students, parents, community members, business leaders, and policymakers to address the question of purpose... You might have better luck asking, 'What is the meaning of life?'"[2]

I would have to agree with that statement wholeheartedly. For every person I have asked this question (and I have asked a lot) I have received a different answer. There are definitely some common underlying themes, but nothing close to consensus. And, in reality, I believe that is because education *does* serve diverse purposes and, ultimately, is a tool that's use is very personal.

So, instead of declaring one overarching purpose to education, let's take a look at a number of them and observe how well formal educational institutions do at meeting each one.

Defining the Purpose

After quite a bit of research and numerous conversations with a diverse group of people, I have found that most people's explanations

3

of the purpose of education fall into four general categories. Education's purpose is to help an individual:

1) Become a lifelong learner
2) Develop character and good citizenry
3) Prepare for the future
4) Lead a happy and fulfilling life

Each category is, of course, full of its own sub-categories. In addition, all four are intricately connected to each other, meaning some overlap is to be expected. Nothing about education (or life for that matter) is so simple that we can just divide its purpose into neat little categories and say we've captured its entire essence. Nevertheless, categories do at least allow us to get our minds around ideas as big as the purpose of education.

Becoming a Lifelong Learner

"Education is not the filling of a pail, but the lighting of a fire."
- William Butler Yeats

Let me highlight that this specific purpose of education is to become a *lifelong* learner. Children are born with an innate drive to learn and do not need to be taught to become learners. Peter Gray – a psychologist, professor and author – explains in his book "Free to Lean" that:

> Children come into the world burning to learn and genetically programmed with extraordinary capacities for learning. They are little learning machines. Within their first four years or so they absorb an unfathomable amount of information and skills without any instruction. They learn to walk, run, jump, and climb. They learn to understand and speak the language of the culture into which they are born, and with that they learn to assert their will, argue, amuse, annoy, befriend, and ask questions. They acquire an incredible amount of knowledge about the physical and social world around them. All of this is driven by their inborn instincts and drives, their innate playfulness and curiosity.[3]

I can personally attest to this miracle of learning; and I am sure that you can too if you have ever been around a small child. I have watched this happen right before my eyes as my son has learned to crawl and then walk, feed himself, say words in both Spanish and English, give hugs and kisses, explore the world around him, pore over books, make messes, clap and wave, climb up and down the stairs, dance, throw balls, color and do things that make his dad and me laugh until we cry. The learning never stops. Everything he does is learning and it is the most fascinating thing to witness.

So the purpose of education is not to teach my son to become a learner. He already is one. I can provide the learning environment, an example, some encouragement and a little bit of guidance, but there's no need to teach my son to become something that is already part of his nature.

What then, is so different about becoming a *lifelong* learner that we need to throw something called "education" into the mix? Honestly, not much. In fact, perhaps the most important purpose of education is to simply ensure that this learning never stops – that this natural drive does not fade, but becomes a lifelong love affair. As parents and educational facilitators, all we really need to do is provide the right learning environments, good examples, some encouragement and a little bit of guidance.

As Peter Gray explains, "Nature does not turn off this enormous desire and capacity to learn when children turn five or six."[3] Consequently, our desire as adults to help refine and sophisticate our child's ability to learn should never hinder their natural drive to grow, explore and understand the world around them. How do we do that?

Several veteran world schooling parents gave me some great insights into the real purpose of education and agreed that the key to becoming a lifelong learner is to become a learner in the present. Brandon Pearce expounded on this idea:

> The purpose is really about presence. If I'm standing in a forest and I'm looking at a leaf, I can just let myself appreciate and say "Wow, this is amazing that this leaf is even here! Look at all the colors! And how did it grow? How did it get here?" If I am just there and present with the leaf and appreciating it, that is going to stir my curiosity into researching botany and into all sorts of different topics. I can learn everything about it that I want to.

Whereas, if I'm forced to look at a biology book and study these things, it's possible that a lot of that knowledge will stick and it may turn into a love for that subject and an appreciation of the leaf and more fuller issues – both sides are important – but, for me, the [most important] aspect is really just getting present and tuning into the beauty that is life itself and letting that fuel my interest and my education, rather than trying to force education to fuel my interests and my own love for life.[4]

As we have discussed, children are already very good at doing this. Have you ever tried going on a walk somewhere with a child without having to stop at least ten times along the way to observe a leaf, play with a bug or jump in a puddle? Kids are naturals at this stuff!

And, perhaps you and I are less skilled at being present simply because we were trained to see education only as something obtained inside a classroom. In our efforts to formalize and mass-produce education, we have taken away our ability to be present in the world. After all, it is rather difficult to allow the world to teach us and drive our natural desire to learn when we've designated only certain times of the day and certain places for learning – especially when those places are inside and isolated from the "real world." Daniel Prince, a world schooling father, touched on this problem when he observed:

Kids in schools these days don't have a love of learning. It's just 'sit down in a classroom with 30 kids, heads down, [be quiet], listen to this, see what I've got on the chalkboard and open your books to page 62.' There's no love there. But if you can give a child a love of learning [so] that they want to learn… and you can give them the tools to go and learn (which we have now at the touch of a button), then they'll educate themselves.[5]

And he is right, if children have a love of learning and they haven't lost the ability to be present and curious about the world, all they really need from us are a few tools and a little bit of guidance. In that sense, the purpose of education – at least in terms of becoming a lifelong learner – is simply to help maintain the childlike curiosity with which we were all born. And we will be much more effective at helping our children maintain that curiosity and love of learning if we have maintained those same qualities in ourselves.

This is not to say that we should just let our children run loose and do whatever they want. The guidance and tools that we provide as parents and teachers are very important, but they do not always have to follow the model of a formal classroom or long lectures. A child may have a natural, burning desire to learn, but we can still help them know how to direct that drive and develop it into something refined and enduring.

To continue with Daniel Prince's advice, the ideal is to "teach through a nurturing, wholistic, hands-on environment to give the student all the tools that they need in order to make their own informed decisions."[5.1] While it may be possible to provide such an environment within a formal educational institution, it is not necessary. You do not need a school to provide your child with this type of education.

In fact, some would argue that many students are better off without the formalities of school. Ben Hewitt, a father, author and unschooler, explains in his book "Home Grown":

> We seem to be afflicted by a cultural belief that if you don't compel people to learn, they will choose not to learn. This belief is rooted in the fallacy that people are inherently lazy and disinterested. It is rooted in the misconception that a child can choose to not learn.

> Indeed, I have found that the truth is exactly the opposite. When you allow people– both children and adults– the freedom to learn what they want, when they want, they come to their learning with fierce passion and energy. They come to it not because they are motivated to make money but because they are driven by something far more powerful than material gain: love of knowledge and the very process of attaining knowledge.

> The result is that they end up learning and doing what they should be learning and doing, when they should be learning and doing it, and for this simple reason they become better at whatever occupation they have chosen, whether it is farmer, lawyer, doctor, mechanic, carpenter, artist, logger, and even teacher. And the world becomes better for it (p.153).[6]

In summary, becoming a lifelong learner is one of the great and noble purposes of education. We educate to provide our children with the pure joy of learning. It is part of what makes us human and makes us feel alive. Consequently, it is a part of our nature that we cannot afford to turn off or ignore, for either ourselves or our children.

Developing Character and Good Citizenry

"You will ever remember that all the end of study is to make you a good man and a useful citizen." – John Adams

One of the great hallmark purposes of education throughout the centuries has been to create individuals of character and good citizenship who are capable of contributing to the society in which they live. All societies have a logical and vested interest in the character of their citizens. Individuals of good character create strong homes and communities. Likewise, educated citizens contribute to society in valuable ways, from eliminating disease to creating jobs to elevating our souls through the arts.

Because of its ability to help individuals develop character and commitment to community, education is a powerful tool for laying the foundation upon which a society can flourish. The educational reformer of the early twentieth century, John Dewey, explained that "Any education is, in its forms and methods, an outgrowth of the needs of the society in which it exists."[7] This, as we'll see, can be a two-edged sword. Societies can be both good and bad, meaning that the various agendas they push undoubtedly bleed into educational policies and practices – for better or worse.

Much good can come from having society as a whole interested in your children and the quality of their character. As long as the values taught correspond with our own, there's not much reason to complain when it comes to harnessing the resources of governmental and educational institutions to teach virtues and values.

The home will always be the most powerful institution for imparting good morals, but on the whole, I think we can agree that there is a positive side to viewing the purpose of education as a means to creating individuals of character who can contribute to society. Education would seem like a hollow endeavor if we failed to instill in our children some degree of kindness and compassion, honesty, respect for diversity, a belief in equality, and the ability to participate in a democracy.[8]

In her 1930 article *Good Citizenship: The Purpose of Education,* Eleanor Roosevelt explained her own outlook on the subject:

> What is the purpose of education? This question agitates scholars, teachers, statesmen, every group, in fact, of thoughtful men and women. The conventional answer is the acquisition of knowledge, the reading of books, and the learning of facts. Perhaps because there are so many books and the branches of knowledge in which we can learn facts are so multitudinous today, we begin to hear more frequently that the function of education is to give children a desire to learn and to teach them how to use their minds and where to go to acquire facts when their curiosity is aroused. Even more all-embracing than this is the statement made not long ago, before a group of English headmasters, by the Archbishop of York, that "the true purpose of education is to produce citizens."[9]

She goes on to explain that she would have children "see how government departments are run and what are their duties, how courts function, what juries are, what a legislative body is and what it does." All of this and more, she explains, so that a child can understand the workings of the nation and the world to see how their own "life and environment fit into the pattern and where his own usefulness may lie."[9]

While she argues that the best place to learn good citizenship is in school because it is a miniature society, this is not the only place or means by which citizenship can be taught. In fact, many children are capable of and would benefit more by participating directly in society (at least with the guidance of his or her parents). I learned more about democracy by going to a town hall meeting with my parents as a pre-teen than I ever did learning to memorize the pre-amble to the Constitution in sign language in elementary school.

Once again, schools can do a decent job of teaching character and good citizenry, but that does not mean it cannot be taught more powerfully or effectively in the home or by some other method.

And that brings me back to the idea of the two-edged sword of society's interest in molding its citizens through education: it makes education political. Even in the most well-governed nations,

9

government-run schools teach what the government dictates. Of course, there are many fabulous educators out there who bring their unique views and personality to the classroom, including those willing to deviate from the politically correct path. I enjoyed being taught by many of them.

Still, one of the major reasons I decided to go to a private university was because I was so tired of the little dance around the truth my teachers were forced to do every so often simply because of what was allowed to be taught and what was not. I wanted to learn truth, not just what was politically correct.

Unfortunately, if we look at the origins of our formal educational system, we quickly discover that it was not created to serve such a purpose. In his book "The One World Schoolhouse", Khan Academy founder Salman Khan explains:

> It may come as a surprise to learn that all [the] then-radical innovations in what we now call K-12 education were first put in place in eighteenth-century Prussia. Compulsory, tax-supported public education was seen as a political at least as much as a pedagogical tool, and no apology was made for this.
>
> The idea was not to produce independent thinkers, but to churn out loyal and tractable citizens who would learn the value of submitting to the authority of parents, teachers, church, and, ultimately, king.
>
> However, whether it was intentional or not, the system tended to stifle deeper inquiry and independent thought. In the 1800s, high-level creative and logical thinking may not have been as important as a disciplined tractability coupled with basic skills, but two hundred years later, they clearly are (p.76-77).[10]

Education can be a powerful thing for whatever end it is made to serve. In Prussia it was designed to teach obedience to authority. And while obedience to good laws and the proper authority is a moral character we need to promote in our society, it should not be the sole purpose of any educational system – especially at the expense of deeper thinking and creativity.

I do not say this to insinuate that the teachers in the system are actively trying to teach passivity and blind obedience to authority. And

I'm not saying that they aren't trying to teach deeper thinking or inspire creativity. What I am saying is that the system does not allow much flexibility for such things.

In fact, besides wanting to spend more time with my baby, one of the biggest reasons I decided to stop teaching was because I simply hadn't found a way to bend the system enough to teach the way I felt my students could actually learn. I wanted them to be able to fail and explore, to try new things and pursue their passions, but instead I was stuck writing tests, grading worksheets and disciplining children who I knew were perfectly capable of learning outside of such a rigid environment. And I know many other wonderful educators who echo those sentiments of displeasure with the system.

So, if we are telling ourselves that we need to send our children to formal schools because it is the only way they can participate in a mini society and learn its essential values, I would say we are selling ourselves and our children short. Developing citizens of character is a very important purpose of education, but I find it difficult to believe that the Prussian model upon which our schools largely function will help our children become the kind of citizens we need in the 21st century.

Our ever-globalizing world needs citizens who are just as global. Our complex societies need individuals who can think deeply and create solutions in a constantly changing world. If we expect our children to contribute to the world, we cannot continue to teach them inside a model designed for the eighteenth century meant to create passive subjects and submissive factory workers.[10]

We need to transform our current educational model if we are to fully achieve this important purpose of education. In 1991, the environmental educator David Orr said,

> Education is no guarantee of decency, prudence, or wisdom. More of the same kind of education will only compound our problems... The worth of education must now be measured against the standards of decency and human survival... It is not education that will save us, but education of a certain kind...
>
> The plain fact is that the planet does not need more "successful" people. But it does desperately need more peacemakers, healers, restorers, storytellers, and lovers of every shape and form. It needs people who live well in their places. It

needs people of moral courage willing to join the fight to make the world habitable and humane. And these needs have little to do with success as our culture has defined it.[11]

With that in mind, if we are to view moral character and good citizenship as the purpose of education, let us first define the kind of character and citizenship that will not only help us to better ourselves, our communities and our nations but also enable our children to become global citizens capable of making a difference in the world. If we can do that, we are well on our way to achieving this vital purpose of education.

Preparing for the Future

"Education is our passport to the future, for tomorrow belongs only to the people who prepare for it today." - Malcom X

What do we mean when we say the purpose of education is to prepare our children for the future? And what kind of future are we talking about? Does that future have to specifically include college? If so, is the aim of a K-12 education to prepare for college? Or should education aim at preparing someone for a future career? What about teaching life skills such as cooking a balanced meal or managing family finances? Perhaps we mean all of those things and more.

In general, viewing education as a means to prepare for the future is a natural instinct we have as parents to prepare our children for independence. Nancy Sathre-Vogel, a world schooling mother whose sons have now left the nest, had this to say about the purpose of education:

> We talk a lot about how the purpose of education is to prepare kids for the world that comes. We go through childhood just like all animals. Some animals are born with survival skills and other animals [need] their mothers to take care of them until they develop their wings and can fly away. So, [to an extent], the purpose of childhood is to get one ready to head out on their own. Education is just part of that.
>
> I don't like to say that the goal of education is to prepare one for adulthood... but I do think that there is something to that

idea in that we are setting the stage and helping kids learn the skills that they will need to be successful on their own.[12]

I would have to agree. It is nice to talk about becoming lifelong learners and developing individuals of character – and those are undoubtedly valid and important purposes of education – but most of us would probably feel our educational efforts had failed us to at least a small degree if they did not prepare us for the financial responsibilities and adult realities of the future.

That is really what hit me on my graduation night. I realized that, for the most part, my formal education had done a decent job of fueling my love of learning and promoting good morals and citizenship (although a lot of credit has to go to my parents on both counts as well). I even felt prepared for college, but life outside of the classroom (you know, out there in the "real world") was something for which I felt entirely unprepared.

It wasn't that I did not have a killer set of life skills in my arsenal, it was just that I did not feel confident using them in the real world. The connection between what I had learned in school and how those concepts and formulas could be used outside the classroom was rather foggy; and the divide was just a little bit overwhelming.

How did calculus solve problems in real life? Who actually used chemistry unit conversions in their day-to-day work? On the more practical side of things, when was it appropriate to ask for a raise? And how could I know how much my work was worth, anyway? No one had taught me those things in school. And to make matters worse, no one was going to be there to give me an "A+" for a job well done so I could know that I was doing the whole "life" thing correctly.

In all, the fault was not in how well the formal education system had taught me the concepts. I had the concepts down pat. The problem – like I mentioned before – was that I couldn not connect my knowledge to anything practical. As Salman Khan points out, this is due in large part to the way in which subjects are presented in isolation from each other in the traditional school system:

> It would certainly seem… that the most effective way to teach would be to emphasize the flow of a subject, the chain of associations that relates one concept to the next and across subjects. Unfortunately, however, the standard approach to classroom teaching does just the opposite. This is most

obviously seen in the artificial separation of traditional academic subjects. We lop them off at ultimately arbitrary places; ...

The breaking up of concepts like these has profound and even crucial consequences for how deeply students learn and how well they remember (p. 48) ... In our misplaced zeal for tidy categories and teaching modules that fit neatly into a given length of class time, we deny students the benefit– the physiological benefit– of recognizing connections.

The conventional educational approach tends to be drearily consistent; take a piece of a subject and treat it as if it existed in a vacuum. Spend one or three or six weeks of classroom lectures on it, then give a test and move on. No wonder so many students acknowledge that they largely forget a subject soon after they've been tested on it. Well, why shouldn't they forget? (p.50)[10]

As far as traditional schools go, it is very hard to work against this system. Units and subjects and classroom lectures are too convenient to just throw out with the trash. They allow for organized timelines and teachers with specialized knowledge. The problem, of course, is that learning is not an organized process. It is personal. And, as much as we want to standardize it so we can evaluate student progress, learning will never be effective as a one-size-fits-all endeavor.

At least, not if we want every student to be adequately prepared for the future. Alan Singer, a professor and member of the New York State Council for the Social Studies put it this way:

One thing [... we] never address is that maybe the American school system is working the way it is intended to work. It sorts people out in school preparing them to be sorted out in life. It prepares some people for power, influence, and wealth convincing them that they earned their extravagant rewards based on hard work and merit rather than luck or privilege... Is the purpose of a public education system to provide a selected few with a pathway to attain wealth, influence, and power?[8]

If it is, then the system is working just fine. In a recent study, it was found that "while the performance of the country's highest achievers is increasing... the lowest performing students are performing worse than ever."[13]

This, surprisingly, comes at a time when high school graduation rates have risen to over 80% – an incredible achievement, for sure. The catch, of course, is that only 40% of those high school graduates are considered ready for college-level work. Government programs and standardized testing raised the statistics bar for schools, but states found they could get the higher graduation rates simply by lowering the standard for graduation.[8] Instead of improving education, these tests and programs have only managed to "dumb down" education so more people can have a little piece of paper saying they made it through the system.

I saw the results of this phenomenon first hand as a teaching assistant for a freshman course at my university. For that particular freshman class, one in every eight students was a valedictorian in high school. Very impressive. However, while I loved my students greatly, every time I sat down to grade their essay assignments I couldn't help but wonder, "Who taught (or failed to teach) these students how to write?" There were definitely some students who knew what they were doing, but it was a rather sobering experience to realize just how many of them did not know how to communicate their ideas on paper. How was this possible?

And it is not just writing that seems to be slipping past our nation's students. In the previously mentioned study, they found that "only about a third of U.S. high school seniors are prepared for college-level coursework in math and reading."[13] The numbers are even less encouraging when it comes to life skills. A shocking 70% of young people do not know how to sew on a button,[14] over 50% do not know how to change a tire,[15] and 20% or more have never washed their own clothes or shopped for their own food (and 11% do not even know how to cook that food).[16]

I do not point out all of these things just to bemoan the state of today's youth, I do so to recognize the fact that there is no guarantee that the system will adequately raise your children for you. I doubt that is what our current educational system was ever designed to do – or what we would ever want it to do. And, even if the powers that be decided to completely usurp that all-important parental role, it seems quite obvious at present that they are not at all qualified for the job.

15

You are responsible for your child's growth, education and preparation for the future. Do not be afraid to fulfill that role!

Formal educational institutions are not doing a stellar job at preparing students with college and life skills. They are doing some good, but it appears that it is not enough. But do we still need them to prepare students for the wonderful world of work?

For many, high school is merely a stepping stone to college where the real preparation and networking needed to launch a successful career can happen. This, many argue, is the purpose of a college education. I am not going to claim that college does not enable people to learn important concepts, gain essential skills and develop crucial relationships. It does. But if we are only looking at the purpose of a high school and college education as a means to preparing for a future career, the statistics tell a rather sad story.

Aside from the crushing amounts of debt many college graduates have to deal with, getting a job with a college degree these days is, unfortunately, very difficult. In his book "The End of Jobs", Taylor Pearson points out some of the rather painful facts:

> More than half of America's recent college graduates are either unemployed or working in a job that doesn't require a bachelor's degree. In 2014, the overall employment rate for law school graduates fell for the sixth consecutive year. It would appear that knowledge is no longer the scarce resource it was one hundred years ago. Yet credentialism, a system for measuring knowledge, has continued to grow dramatically. The number of college graduates has been climbing steadily since the 1940s and shows no signs of slowing down.[17]

However, as he goes on to explain, the astounding growth in the number of college graduates does not seem to be paying off. He offers a new solution to this dilemma that we'll look at in a minute, but first let's examine an equally important point he brings up: credentialism. Credentialism is part of what economists like to refer to as signaling. The more credentials you have in the form of degrees, good grades, certifications, etc. the more power you have to signal to employers that you are qualified for the job.

In a world of imperfect information where employers have little to go on to determine the potential contributions you can make to their business, the more credentials you have, the easier it is for them to guess at the level of skills, commitment and knowledge you possess. Ivy League institutions, for example, are assumed to bestow greater skills and deeper knowledge, making their degrees more valuable credentials than, say, a degree from your local community college. Of course, this system is flawed.

And, as more and more people follow the path of credentialism, the less potent those factory-produced diplomas become. (Just ask all those unemployed college graduates.) And all this at a time when student debt is skyrocketing. Granted, college graduates are much more likely to be employed than someone without a degree, so this is not a vote to kick higher education to the curb. Again, it is a call to rethink the value we place on the way things have always been done and to get creative with how we approach education in general.

The financial writer Charles Hugh Smith argues that an entirely new feedback loop of accreditation is needed that does not rely on signaling. Instead, you should find ways to accredit yourself by proving your skills with real world knowledge and experiences that are valued in the field you intend to enter.[18]

And he is not the only one advocating a new approach. Salman Khan has envisioned a whole new college experience that revolves around real world internships and mentoring programs like those run by Google and Microsoft. These internships would be accompanied by student paced learning void of the typical lecture style teaching format. And where testing is required to know the limits of a potential employee's knowledge, instead of GPAs and diplomas, employers would administer tests specific to the needs of their company (p.229-235).[10]

Others, however, have the confidence that many of today's young people are more than capable of making a living for themselves without the aid of a college education. Peter Thiel (the founder of PayPal and Palantir Technologies and the first outside investor in Facebook) has begun the Thiel Fellowship, which rewards qualifying recipients with a $100,000 grant to skip or leave college and pursue their own ideas with the aid and support of successful founders, investors and scientists in the Thiel Foundation.

This vision of the future corresponds with Taylor Pearson's arguments about the value of entrepreneurship in a shifting economy where knowledge alone is not enough to ensure a financially secure future. He points out that,

Just as college and graduate school emerged over the course of the twentieth century as a clear path to a job, life paths and social scripts for entrepreneurship are emerging that make the path clearer (p.15).

The social and technological inventions of the past one hundred years have brought us to the "End of Jobs" while making entrepreneurship safer, more accessible, and more profitable than ever (p.51).[17]

However we choose to look at it, if we consider education's main responsibility to be preparation for the future, we need to rethink and restructure the typical pathway to career success, or at least take a very conscious, active approach within the existing systems. If we can help our children take responsibility for this process, they will ultimately have control over the path their life is going to take... which is probably what we really mean when we say we want to prepare our kids for the future anyway.

Leading a Fulfilling and Happy Life

"Educating the mind without educating the heart, is no education at all." - Aristotle

This final purpose of education can be, in a sense, the result of the three that we have already discussed. After all, if we maintain our love of learning, are people of good character who contribute to society and manage to obtain a personally satisfying degree of financial security, then we are well on our way to leading a happy and fulfilling life. However, this particular category has enough of its own distinct characteristics that it deserves its own explanation.

Beyond its societal and financial benefits, education is a critical factor of *personal* well-being. And, as we have discussed before, this must be education of a certain kind. If we are not careful, we may end up trading time in school for our children's overall well-being. In his book "Free to Learn", Peter Gray observes the correlation between the decline in children's play time over the years and the increase in stress-related mental disorders. He admits that correlation does not prove causation, but argues that a strong logical case can be built to explain such a relationship (p.17).[3]

Think about it, in many places school days have become longer, school years have been extended, and the average homework load has increased so much that children have very little time to be children. Kindergarten has become the new first grade and – where only a decade ago 15% of kindergarteners were readers – in many school districts with full-day attendance requirements, 90% of kindergarteners can now read.[19]

This should be celebrated, right? We are making huge strides in education, aren't we? Faster is better, isn't it? After all, the world is becoming ever more competitive and any advantage we can give our children is desirable, especially when so many students are entering college totally unprepared for the work that will be required of them. Or maybe not.

A study co-authored by Professor Thomas S. Dee of Stanford found that "delaying kindergarten for one year reduced inattention and hyperactivity by 73 percent for an average child at age 11, … and it virtually eliminated the probability that an average child at that age would have an 'abnormal,' or higher-than-normal rating for the inattentive-hyperactive behavioral measure."[59] The conclusion? *Delaying* kindergarten and prolonging childhood play aids mental health development that will benefit the child far into the future.

Maybe, just *maybe*, it is the attitude of learning as a race to the top that is the real problem.

Perhaps we are pushing so hard that learning has become work to be avoided. We have stamped out the joy of learning and stolen away the precious hours of childhood in pursuit of an education that will prepare our children for a future of success as the world sees it. And in that effort we have forgotten that, at the end of the day, what we really want for our children is that they have happy, fulfilling lives.

Have we confused academic and career success with happiness? Obviously, such things can form part of a happy and fulfilling life, but if we stop and think about what we really want for our children, I doubt we would actually want them to be successful at the expense of their happiness. As Peter Gray points out,

> The world is full of unhappy lawyers, doctors, and business executives, and many clerks and janitors are happy, fulfilled, and decent. Career success is not life success. You can be happy or unhappy in any profession, but you can't be happy, at

least not for long stretches, if you feel that your life is not yours (p.222).[3]

To that extent, education as a means toward happiness and fulfillment must give children the power to direct their own lives. Unfortunately, the traditional educational pattern of adult-directed learning leaves a lot to be desired in that regard.

As we have already seen, our current educational model was originally designed to teach submission and obedience to authority figures who determine what a child learns, when they will learn it and how that learning will occur. It comes as no surprise, then, that many children do not feel that they have control over their life. If they cannot control how they learn – and have little time to do anything else each day – when will they have the chance to direct themselves in any endeavor?

Still, this does not mean that change is impossible. Technology is already enabling teachers to transform the classroom from the traditional pedagogical methods of teacher-directed learning to a more andragogical method typically used for adult learning that is self-directed with the teacher as the guide, instead of the director (p.175-176).[10]

There is also a growing trend among schools to use meditation in the place of detention, or to simply practice mindfulness in the classroom. It seems that teachers and school districts are catching on to the need to teach the whole child and not just their brain. Wholistic teaching that involves helping students mentally, emotionally and even spiritually is certainly becoming more popular and is definitely encouraging. But is it enough?

If you are considering packing your bags and traveling the world, you can easily help your child appreciate such practices as meditation, spirituality, mindfulness and self-directed learning. While it is great that schools are catching on, you do not necessarily need them to help your children obtain an education that will help them live a happy and fulfilling life. In fact, traveling may just give your child the exact experiences and environments they need to understand their place in the world and what it really means to them to be happy.

As Ben Hewitt expresses it: "The truth is there are so many permutations of what it means to live a good life, and I often wonder if all I really want for my children is the ability to determine which permutation is right for them (p.61)."[6]

Chapter Two: The Path
What Do Children *Really* Need to Know?

Someone once told me that I would never want to see how sausages are made. "They're delicious," he said, "but once you've seen what goes into them, you won't want to eat another one for as long as you live."

I felt the same way about school when I began teaching. Granted, I did not actually have a teaching license and had not studied to become a teacher, but the schools in Mexico are not that demanding of English teachers if you are a native speaker with some informal background in teaching and a willingness to give English classes.

During college I had studied education in relation to the development of nations and its power to lift people out of poverty. And, before my life completely changed and brought me to Mexico, I had planned on working with Teach for America to gain on-the-ground experience as a real teacher and get perspective for when I became a high-browed educational policy maker.

Funny how life changes. And yet, here I was in Mexico doing exactly what I had hoped to do in the United States. Even better, I was actually out there, in the world, getting the same on-the-ground experience I had hoped to gain in the US, but with the international perspective I actually wanted.

And so began my teaching experience. I felt like I had snuck my way into the education factory to see how learning happens from the adult's perspective. As a kid, I had adored my teachers (and I still do). Learning was magical and the teachers who seemed to make it all happen had to be some of the most amazing people on the planet. And they were.

However, for some reason, I had always thought that there was a profound rationale behind why we were taught state history in fourth grade, U.S. history in fifth grade and world history in another. I honestly thought there was something scientific about the development of my young mind that meant I had to learn about the five senses in first grade. Imagine my utter surprise when I realized that there really is no rhyme or reason to why we teach what we teach when we teach it.

They had let me into the factory and now I could see everything that goes into formal education. And just like the effects of seeing how a sausage is made, I was not in love with the process. Plenty of really good things were going on and learning was definitely happening all over the place, but I could not believe just how arbitrary it all was.

Why would my students read this book and not that one? Because I decided that was what we would do. Why would we learn about caterpillars and butterflies during this unit? Because that was what came in the textbook. Why would my middle school students watch the musical, *Annie*, today? Aside from the connection to the current unit on music and the opportunity to practice listening, it was because I was pregnant and too tired to do anything else. Shocking, really.

Part of me cringes at the recognition that I was probably not the absolute greatest teacher that had ever graced a classroom, but another part of me realizes that my childhood trust in the system was just a little bit misplaced.

I received yet more confirmation of this upon reading Nancy Sathre-Vogel's book, "Roadschooling: The Ultimate Guide to Education Through Travel".[20] Nancy is a licensed teacher with years of teaching experience who traveled from Alaska to Argentina with her husband and kids on bikes over a period of four years, world schooling along the way. I sat down and talked with her in preparation for this book and she let me in on a little secret about formal education. She said,

> By convention, we teach the five senses in grade one. It's just what grade one has done for forever and ever and so we do that in grade one. We do the human body in grade five. It's just what we do. We do our community in grade three. In grade four we go to our state. It's just convention. It's just what we've decided to do. Not that we have to do it that way, it's just the way it has developed, it's the way that we've done it. And now a

lot of people are locked into that and they feel that's how it *has* to be done. And my feeling is that it doesn't.

> It doesn't matter what [children] learn, just *that* they learn. The important thing is that there is that love of learning, that they know how to learn [and] if there is a topic that they decide they want to learn about, that they know how to get the information, they know what to do with the information, and that they know how to process that information. So I don't care what they learn, just *that* they learn. That's the key part.[12]

And it is true; until we find something that we want to specialize in, most of the topics that we cover in school are just superficial learning. I do not mean superficial in the sense that the things taught in school do not matter or have no depth, but rather that the topics are mostly there to teach the deeper purposes we discussed in Chapter One and the broader skills needed to achieve them. Beyond the basics, the subjects, topics, units, projects, and reports are mostly just tools available to help children learn how to learn.

Now, one of the main concerns you have probably heard from people when you have mentioned your interest in taking your kids out of school to travel the world probably goes along the lines of, "But how will your kids ever learn all the things they would learn in school?" A question like this usually involves the underlying assumption that children can only learn in school and that schools are the all-knowing institutions we believed them to be as children. Schools, under this assumption, are where 'learning happens' and where everything that a child needs to know is carefully crafted into the optimal conditions for learning.

From my own experience, as well as Nancy's and many others, I can assure you that this is not necessarily true. The topics covered in formal educational institutions are more arbitrary than you might suspect. So, when your friends, family members and complete strangers question your parental judgment, just remind yourself that the system is not as perfect as they imagine it to be. They might not know that, but you do. So take a breath and move forward.

Questions of this nature do, however, tend to beg another question: What do children *really* need to know?

We have already discussed the purpose of education in terms of its various end goals, but what exactly do children need to learn along their educational path to get to those goals? If you are considering becoming a world schooling family, chances are you will not be relying on a school to teach your kids everything they need to know. As such, you are going to need to know the answer to this question. So... what do children *really* need to know?

What Children Do Not Need

Before we get too far ahead of ourselves, let's back up a bit and first figure out what it is that children do not need from their academic pursuits. It will be a lot easier to define what they actually need when we have cleared out all of the shiny objects and fluff that so often get in the way of learning.

1) It is not about knowing 'stuff'

We have touched on this already, but it is important to remind ourselves that memorizing information is mostly just part of the superficial aspects of education. If we are not using the information as a means to a greater end or in connection with the bigger picture, then the acquisition of information is a limited endeavor. Brandon Pearce explained it this way:

I find that while there is so much that you can learn in the world – so much history and chemistry and all sorts of different topics that will make you a well-rounded, intelligent person able to contribute to society – I also believe that we live in a world where we don't need information. We're so flooded with information; anything we want to know is at our fingertips with Google. So, the more important thing is to know how to live joyfully and how to live with kindness.

[History and chemistry] are important, but we can't learn everything. So, if you're interested in chemistry, then dive into. If not, just get the basics. I don't need to know chemistry to contribute to society in my own way. There are people who are super passionate about [chemistry] and they will do that. For me, I've got other interests. It's perfectly fine to specialize in the interests that call to you and get just a general understanding of all the rest, which will come naturally.[4]

Do not worry so much about how well your child can commit dates and facts to memory. Instead, focus on the more important skills and characteristics they will need to use such information to positive and productive ends.

2) It is not about performances and tests

I am going to go out on a limb here and delve into physics for a second to make an analogy about education. In quantum mechanics, the Heisenberg Uncertainty Principle explains how we can never know an object's exact position and exact speed at the same time. As Heisenburg himself explained it, "the more precisely the position is determined, the less precisely the momentum is known, and conversely."[21]

In a sense, the more we focus on one thing, the harder it is to focus on the other. To a certain extent, we can apply this same principle to education – specifically, to testing and student potential. According to Salman Khan,

> Tests say little or nothing about a student's potential to learn a subject. At best, they offer a snapshot of where the student stands at a given moment in time. Since... students learn at widely varying rates, and... catching on faster does not necessarily imply understanding more deeply, how meaningful are these isolated snapshots? (p.91)[10]

In other words, we may be able to say with precision what a student knows at a given moment in time, but that measurement tells us little about the student's momentum and ultimate potential. Conversely, if we completely write off tests and only focus on the optimistic and limitless potential of a student, we may shortchange our ability to identify important gaps in their learning that can easily be fixed.

Tests, then, are not to be despised simply because they exist. They have their virtues. The problem, of course, is when we get so focused on testing that we completely lose focus on actual learning. And, unfortunately, the pendulum seems to swing more in that direction. Since it is so difficult to measure true learning, Peter Gray argues that,

> What matters in today's educational world is performance that can be scored and compared across students, across schools,

and even across nations to see who is better and who is worse. Knowledge that is not part of the school curriculum, even deep knowledge, doesn't count (p.9).[3]

In the end, children and true learning are the casualties of such attitudes toward tests and education. The world gets cheated in the process as well. The world needs creative minds who can think and find solutions outside the box, and that is difficult to inspire in a system that tends to teach to the test.

If we are honest about it, we would admit that standardized tests are not made for students. Hewitt states that, "If there is value in the standardized, performance-based curriculums utilized by the vast majority of schools, that value is realized primarily by the institutions themselves and by the economic and social structures that are fed by standardized learning (p.55)."[6] Children do not need standardized tests, educational institutions do. But the more these institutions focus on testing as an end unto itself, the less our children benefit.

Children do not *really* need to master rote memorization or to know all the artificially segregated concepts required for standardized tests in order to become lifelong learners, develop good character, prepare for the future or live happy and fulfilling lives. So, while some tests are desirable for diagnosing gaps and guiding learning, we do not need them the way that standardized tests currently operate within our institutions of learning.

3) Children do not need segregated subjects

We already covered this in Chapter One, so I will be brief. Ultimately, children need to see the connections. Segregating concepts is not the way of the natural world and doing so isolates them from the realities in which they need to be understood.

Finland is setting the example for exactly this type of unsegregated learning. Already one of the beacons of light among the world's public education systems, Finland is overhauling its entire method of teaching. By 2020, they plan to phase out individual subjects in favor of teaching according to "broad phenomena".[22] It is encouraging to see that some educational institutions understand the need for change and are acting accordingly.

It may take a while for all of them to figure it out though, so I would not wait for the system to fix the problems in traditional education for you.

What Children *Do* Need

Now that we have covered the negatives, let's turn to the positives and what kids *really* need to know to excel in learning, work and life. Honestly, there is no one answer to this question. This is a big topic with infinite answers, but let's try and simplify again to at least get a proximate idea of what children need to learn. The basics involve:

- The intelectual
- The social
- The personal
- The practical
- The creative and
- The global

The Intellectual

The most basic intellectual foundation for any child is that of the traditional "Three R's": reading, writing, and arithmetic. While they sound rudimentary, these skills are vital infrastructure for any future intellectual construction.

With them, children will be able to investigate and test explanations, construct their own explanations and engage in argument from evidence. They will be able to obtain, evaluate and communicate information as they make sense of an ever-changing world.[23]

Best of all, these skills can be learned outside the classroom "with surprisingly little effort, and in a surprisingly scant amount of time, and always in the context of a child's true interests and passions (p.150)."[6]

Here is what a couple of world school moms had to say about the importance of reading, writing and arithmetic as a foundation for their children's learning:

Jennifer Miller

At a very basic level, [children] need to have an understanding of how the world works (which is science, culture, history), they need to have the ability to communicate so that they can change the world in whatever way they end up being passionate about doing (so that means that they need to be able to read and write well and express themselves), and they need to be able to run a business so that they can live their lives and be successful (which means math).

If you're at a point where you can be financially secure and independent, then you have a lot of freedom in this world to do a lot of things that really matter. Our goal for our kids is that they be excellent communicators, that they have a real deep understanding of the world and how it works, and that they are equipped to be adults and run their lives. [And that means] in terms of their businesses, and not necessarily just the ability to do a job, but the ability to think outside the box and create their own rain, if you will.[24]

Nancy Sathre-Vogel

[The most important skills are] the process skills: reading, writing and being able to manipulate numbers. If you can read, write and manipulate numbers you are good to go. It doesn't matter if you learn the phases of the moon or the parts of the flower, it doesn't matter if you understand any of the content. None of that matters. Whether you learn about the Revolutionary War or the Civil War or the Egyptian War, it doesn't matter. None of the content matters. What matters is that you know how to read, you know how to write, and you are able to manipulate numbers fluently. If you can do that and have a love of learning, then you're good. You're golden![12]

Building on the "Three R's", it is important to develop critical thinking skills, as well as basic logic and problem solving. This also means teaching our children to ask questions about everything and learn to never take anything at face value. This also brings up the importance of curiosity as an intellectual skill. Curiosity causes us to not only ask questions about why things are the way they are, but to also define problems that need to be solved.[23]

Another important intellectual skill for the 21st century is that of digital or technological literacy. For the most part, kids naturally learn how to use technology. Peter Gray explains that,

> Children are naturally motivated to play… at new skills that lie at the culture's cutting edge. Because of this, children typically learn to use new technology faster than do their parents. From an evolutionary perspective, that is no accident. At a gut, genetically based level, children recognize that the most crucial skills to learn are those that will be of increasing importance in the future – the skills of their own generation, which may be different from those of their parents' generation. The value of this attraction to the new is especially apparent in modern times, when technology and the skills required to master that technology change so rapidly (p.125).[3]

As parents, we can teach our children the appropriate limits and uses of technology when necessary and encourage our children to learn as much as they can about how different technologies work and affect society.

Additionally, it is increasingly important to give our children an understanding of how the world works. In traditional schools this would be identified by the segregated scientific subjects: the natural sciences of biology, physics, chemistry, and environmental awareness, as well as the social sciences of history, government, economics and geography, etc. With this understanding of the world and how it works, we can also teach social responsibility and ethics.

The final skill I will include in this section is that of language. And by language I mean learning a second or third or even more languages. The workplaces of the future (and today) will need individuals who have a deep understanding and practical ability to use foreign languages. This, of course, requires experience and immersion, not just classroom learning.

This type of learning will be much easier for families that are traveling the world and immersing their children in foreign languages. In fact, we will talk later about strategies for families who have this specific skill in mind as an end goal of their child's education.

The Social

One of the biggest objections I have heard to the various forms of homeschooling over the years is that it does not allow children the opportunity to gain important social skills. And I will be the first to admit that I agreed with that logic for a long time. However, this is one belief that – through personal experience – I learned was misguided.

Some of my best friends in the world grew up being homeschooled. Once they reached middle school age, however, they chose to attend public school. From the moment they walked through the school doors, they were making friends left and right. They were happy and sociable and bright; quite the opposite of the socially awkward homeschool stereotype. In fact, it wasn't long before my homeschooled friends had formed a tight-knit and very large group of incredible friends that has endured to this day.

Although I had been in the public school system since I was five years old, it was my friends who had been homeschooled who were able to converse with ease, involve everyone around them and effortlessly create community. I was humbled (and very grateful for their superior social skills).

A recent study gave me some insight into how my friends' social skills were so superior to mine, despite their many years out of the public education system. Researchers from Pennsylvania State University and Duke University found that career success could be predicted as early as kindergarten, and all based on correlations with a child's social skills.[25]

Interestingly, the study states that these correlations can be observed "as early as" kindergarten, but this is only because the participants' assessments *began* in kindergarten. As such, I have a sneaking suspicion that if they were observed earlier on, it would be quite easy to discover that the participants did not learn their social skills starting on their first day of kindergarten.

In fact, chances are they learned a lot of their social skills from home. Social skills are first learned from parents, siblings, other relatives, people within the community and through playing freely with other children. So, believe it or not, factors beyond public school can determine a child's sociability – I would even say that they matter more.

It is important to note, however that not every homeschooled child will have the social skills of my dear friends. And even they craved the social environment that a school provides in order to let those skills flourish. In some cases, a child will greatly benefit from a structured school setting with plenty of social opportunities. As the parent, be willing to recognize when your child needs more socialization and look for ways to encourage social skills, whether in a formal school setting or through an alternative solution.

On a more practical note, what kind of social skills do children need to develop? The previously mentioned study observed how the kindergarteners interacted in terms of unprompted peer cooperation, helpfulness, understanding each other's feelings and resolving problems on their own. The results found that socially competent children (according to their definition) were much more successful in terms of college and employment, and those with limited social skills were more likely to binge drink, apply for public housing and get arrested.[25]

So, along with reading, writing and arithmetic, teach by example and give your child opportunities to learn social skills such as collaboration and teamwork, compassion, communication, leadership, service and an appreciation for diversity. This can come by giving your children time to play and socialize with other children, as well as by watching *you* socialize with the people you meet along the way.

And, if you are still worried that your kids will not learn these social skills as they are traveling the globe with you, here is what Daniel Prince had to say about the topic:

> What we noticed the most — and this is the thing that most people would ask us when we would introduce ourselves and say that we were world schooling/homeschooling — they'd just get hung up on [the homeschooling] immediately. They wouldn't say "What! You're traveling the world? That's amazing!" They would just hone in on the homeschool comment. "You what? You homeschool?" And they would look at you like you're some kind of freak and you're an irresponsible parent. You could feel the judgement immediately.

> And the first question out of their mouths was always, "But how are they going to socialize? How are they going to grow

up?" Basically, they were saying that you're going to have weird kids. That's an amazing thing to come from somebody who's never done that, but would be happy enough to cast that kind of dispersion.

But what we found is the complete opposite. Our kids are so sociable to the point that adults that we meet will tell us, "We can't believe it. We've just been talking to your kids on the beach for 30 minutes and they are amazing! It's really amazing what they're telling us. They've told us all about your travels. They're so articulate. We're shocked that they would just spark up a conversation with us. So, the whole argument that people put out there that homeschool kids are going to find it hard to socialize is just complete nonsense…

In school, you get into these little cliques – you've got the jocks and the goths and whatever and that's it and that's who you are and you can't talk to the other guys. Whereas, [our kids] will talk to anyone. [They] don't care what you look like or what you're wearing or what color you are or how tall you are or how small you are or how big you are, they just want to reach out and talk. They'll play with any kid out there. So, myth busted on that one![5]

The Personal

However you view the purpose of education, helping children master themselves is an important skill for achieving any worthwhile end. Characteristics and skills such as confidence, commitment, emotional health, relaxation, stress management, and spiritual connection are all important for our children to acquire.

Physical health is another personal skill children can use throughout their life. As parents, we can set good examples and teach the principles of exercise, diet and nutrition, and even the appreciation for recreation and time spent in nature.

In addition, habits are key to much of personal mastery. In one of her many wonderful articles on homeschooling and travel, Jennifer Miller wrote the following about teaching our children how to form good habits:

Before a child turns seven or so, the most important thing you can teach is the formation of good habits. Work on your child's ability to sit and focus for a few minutes at a time on an organized activity that he finds interesting. Work on his ability to have self control and wait patiently. Work on his ability to listen to a progressively longer story being read aloud… and instill these habits as part of daily life. Armed with a tool chest of good habits, your child will be able to teach himself anything, and muster the self discipline to keep working on hard things.[26]

Along with good habits and self discipline comes responsibility. And as Maya Frost points out in her book "The New Global Student", it is our responsibility as parents to move our children toward maturity and autonomy. This is not the school's or society's responsibility, it is ours (p.7).[27] The amazing thing is that our children are very capable of becoming responsible individuals, if only we give them opportunities to BE responsible. Even better news is that those opportunities are abundant in the real world in which you will be taking your globetrotting family.

And responsibility is not the only thing that can be gained while crisscrossing the planet. Flexibility and innovation are two characteristics that are necessary for survival while living life on the road. For those who choose to stay home, these characteristics will be a bit harder to inspire. Maya Frost highlights this dilemma with her own experience in deciding to leave home to travel the world:

Everywhere we looked, parents were intent upon providing secure, consistent living situations that would allow their children to have the same friends, schools, and activities throughout childhood. To us this seemed like a way to promote head-in-the-sand syndrome. Shouldn't we be helping our kids learn how to deal with uncertainty, feel comfortable as outsiders, make new friends, and thrive wherever they go? Or was this just plain mean? Instead of sheltering our kids from the world, we believed we ought to hang a loving life preserver around their necks and toss them into it (p.7-8).

If my husband and I weren't modeling innovation and flexibility—not to mention a 'burb-busting case of boldness—

how could we expect our daughters to develop these qualities for themselves? Showing them that we were willing to look like idiots on a regular basis in order to experience more beauty, freedom, discovery, and fun would give them a brand-new way to view adulthood and their own possibilities (p.10).[27]

Last, but not least, we must encourage our children to take control of their own learning process so that they can develop a personal sense of initiative. In today's world, initiative is critical to success in both work and life. Passively waiting for instructions and knowing how to quickly execute them is a skill lauded in the old factory model workplace of the past. The world does not work like that anymore. We cannot afford to continue teaching such things in schools, and much less as parents. We need to help children own their education. By doing so, they will be much more prepared for life on their own terms.

The Practical

When I was eleven years old, my best friend and I spent the first half of a long summer day canvassing our small town, asking our neighbors if they wanted us to wash their cars. After a particularly long walk down a dusty dirt road, we arrived at the home of one of the nicest ladies in town. We were sure she would let us wash her car (and pay us kindly for it).

Unfortunately, she had just gotten back from the fancy automatic car wash. To say the least, we were disappointed. "But!" she said as we were walking away, "I do have an idea for how you two girls could make a lot of money this summer!"

We returned, eager to hear what she had to say. Her idea turned into one of the most educational opportunities of my life. She explained how she thought it would be a great idea for two young ladies such as ourselves to offer our babysitting services at the town park a few hours every week so the moms in town could have a few hours to themselves during the summer break.

We thought she was brilliant. We left her house in giddy excitement, dropped our car washing tools at the door and spent the rest of the day brainstorming ideas for our little summer babysitting business and daydreaming about the mounds of money we were going to make.

We orchestrated calendars and fun activities for the kids, roped my mom into taking us to the local wholesale store to stock up on snacks and other inventory, distributed flyers to all the families with small children in town, designed and printed business cards that functioned as punchcard passes for our services, and talked the postmaster into letting us advertise our business at the local post office.

I can still remember the sense of empowerment I felt when my mother told my friend and me that we were real entrepreneurs. It was a lot of fun too. Now, we did not end up swimming in mounds of money like Uncle Scrooge McDuck, but we had enough to splurge at the local candy shop on occasion, and by the end of the summer we each had enough money to buy our own clothes for the coming school year.

We ran our business for four summer's straight, and I can tell you with complete certainty that I learned more about business and finances running around the town park with dozens of little kids in tow than I ever did in any finance or business class I took in high school or college. And I am pretty sure that no matter how old I get or how many other things I do, looking back it will always be one of the highlights of my life.

Why do I tell you all of this? Perhaps, in part, to inspire your children's own entrepreneurial endeavors. But, more than anything, I have chosen to disclose this precious childhood memory with you to illustrate the boundless possibilities for teaching our children the practical skills of life. Because, to be honest, practicality is not institutional education's strongpoint.

Job skills are best learned on the job. Basic trade skills are best learned from practicing a trade. Life skills are best learned by living life. And entrepreneurial skills are best learned by, well, entrepreneurship.

So do not be afraid to invite your kids to join you in discussions about the family finances. Let them help you figure out the family budget. And when tax time rolls around, have your kids pull up a seat and learn the stuff hands-on. Do not be afraid to give them work, and if the opportunity for them to take an apprenticeship or internship comes along, go for it. Remember, kids are more capable of responsibility than the world would have you think.

The Creative

The way our modern economy works, "today's world needs a workforce of creative, curious, and self-directed lifelong learners who are capable of conceiving and implementing novel ideas (p.80)"[10] Creativity is a fundamental skill we need to encourage in our children. I say "encourage" and not "teach" because creativity is not really something that can be taught. And more than just encouraging it, we should be careful that our actions do not squelch it. Sir Ken Robinson made this important observation:

> If you're not prepared to be wrong, you'll never come up with anything original... We are now running national education systems where mistakes are the worst things you can make. And the result is that we are educating people out of their creative capacities... We don't grow into creativity, we grow out of it, or rather we get educated out of it.[28]

Also, let me clarify what I mean by creativity. Chances are that the moment you read the word "creativity" you were imagining your child painting a picture or creating some type of art. And that is definitely part of creativity; but we limit our definition of creativity all too much. As Salman Khan points out, "Science, engineering, and entrepreneurship are equally creative (p.219)."[10]

Let us encourage creativity, craftsmanship and imagination on all fronts! Let your kids build, explore and imagine to their hearts content. They will benefit from it more than you know.

The Global

Children *need* a global education. And I do not mean this in the sense of world history and geography. Those topics can definitely form part of a global education, but we have already covered them in the intellectual skills mentioned earlier in this chapter. When I say that children need to learn and acquire global skills, what I mean is actual global experience.

This can come in many ways, shapes and forms (and we will get to those in Section Two of this book). A global education is not just for those who plan to travel the world non-stop their entire lives, but we do need to expand our definition of what qualifies as a satisfactory global education. As Maya Frost explains, "Parents and students need to embrace a definition of "global" that encompasses the notion of becoming knowledgeable of, connected to, and passionately engaged in a world without borders (p.28)."[27]

Beyond the classroom "knowledge of" the world, we need to give our children meaningful opportunities to connect to the world and engage in it. The world has changed too much to ignore it any longer. It used to be that you could grow up in one place and work at the same job your entire life. The world is not like that anymore. We are more connected than ever before and those who know how to operate and contribute to such a world will thrive.

Chapter Three: The Vehicle
Why World Schooling?

Change is a funny thing. In complex economic systems, one change here demands another change there; but such responses are often glacially slow in coming. Because of this, change can be a rather clumsy and disjointed process, often causing (or requiring) anything from mild discomfort to turmoil and destruction along the way.

Revolutions and civil wars, for instance, are the violent outbursts of systems begging for change. And what we have most recently labeled as a global recession is actually the growing pains of a world transitioning between two economic periods.[17]

Such dramatic events tend to be the consequences of resisting change, emphatically forcing us to adapt to the changes around us that we have refused to recognize until then. Yet, even in the face of such extreme consequences, many systems are simply too restrained by their own weight to adequately adjust to the demands of the future in a timely manner.

The good news in all of this is that, as individuals and families, we are quicker and more capable of responding to change than the cumbersome systems that surround us.

This is especially good news when faced with systems that experience no dramatic discomfort capable of forcing needed changes upon them. For example, many people recognize that today's systems of education need to change to better match the world in which we live. However, it is rather unlikely that these systems will face an equivalent of an educational civil war or recession so acute that it will inspire unified, satisfactory change. Salman Khan highlights some of the deep-rooted reasons as to why this is so:

Either for lack of imagination or fear of rocking the boat, the conversation generally stops well short of the kind of fundamental questioning that our educational malaise demands, focusing instead on a handful of familiar but misplaced obsessions like test scores and graduation rates. Those are by no means trivial concerns. Still, what really matters is whether the world will have an empowered, productive, fulfilled population in the generations to come (p.4).

Changing a system of such vast inertia and long tenure is clearly not easy. It's not just that tradition tends to cramp imagination; it's also that our educational system is intertwined with many other customs and institutions. Changing education would therefore lead to changes in other aspects of our society as well. It is my firm belief that over time this would be a very good thing; in the near term, however, such a prospect necessarily suggests disruptions and anxieties (p. 62).

For all its flaws… the standard model has one huge advantage over all other possible education methods: It's there. It's in place. It has tenure. The tendency is to believe that it has to be there. Yet even the briefest survey of the history of education reveals that there is nothing inevitable or preordained about our currently dominant classroom model. Like every other system put in place by human beings, education is an invention, a work in progress. It has reflected, at various periods, the political, economic, and technological realities of its times, as well as the braking power of vested interests.

In short, education has evolved, though not always in a timely manner, or before some unfortunate cohort of young people – a decade's worth? a generation's worth? – has been subjected to obsolete teachings that failed to prepare them for productive and successful futures. It is time – past time – for education to evolve again (p.65).[10]

And I would argue that it is not just time for education to evolve, but rather for it to be transformed into something entirely different. Reforms happen here and there; new ideas pop up all over the place; and yet the system remains largely the same as it did more than a century ago. As Sir Ken Robinson explained, "Every education system in the world is being reformed at the moment and it's not enough. Reform is of no use anymore; because that's simply improving a broken model. What we need... is not an evolution, but a revolution in education."[30]

We need an educational revolution. But that revolution is not going to happen overnight. Where does that leave concerned parents who are ready for a change? Many have found that "the best way to have an impact in the education revolution is to go outside the system."[31] Why wait for the system to change in the unknown, distant future when you can revolutionize your family's education now? In the process, you can help light the path toward the superior educational options that are readily available to prepare future generations for the world they will inherit.

Thanks to our modern era of globalization and technological advancement, it has never been easier than it is now to go outside the system and give our children an incredible education. More importantly, because of globalization and technology, it has never been more crucial that we do so.

While the gap between the way kids are being taught in school and the way they need to learn is growing wider every day, we are at a once-a-millennium turning point capable of revolutionizing education. Those willing to go outside the system will be the first to enjoy the benefits of this new millennial education.

As the rest of the world's educational systems move at their glacial pace of incremental change, you and I (and especially our children) can enjoy the benefits of participating in the education revolution right now.

I believe that the education revolution will one day reach our nations' classrooms. Peter Gray predicts that "In fifty years... educators will see today's approach to schooling as a barbaric relic of the past (p.88)."3.6 But I am not willing to wait fifty years. Are you? I agree with Maya Frost's bottom line:

> Work for change, but please, oh please, do not wait for it. I'm an optimist. I firmly believe that our education system will be radically improved eventually, but we simply can't turn this Big School bus on a dime. And so while that bus is doing a few three-corner maneuvers, it's our responsibility as parents and mentors to make sure that our children or charges do not miss

out on their best opportunities to get a truly international education. Our ed revolution can't wait for the lumbering pace of legislation—we need to kick it into high gear now and pursue it through both personal boldness and community barn raising (p.46).[27]

Joining the Education Revolution

Having said all this, I can already feel the question forming in your mind: How exactly do I spark a family-level education revolution? Good question. It is great to get all fired up about the problems in the system and how we need to change education, but it is an entirely different ballgame to actually do something about it. You know, "Be the change."

Now, many people who pick up this book will already have an idea of how to join the education revolution. Perhaps you already have. But for those still figuring things out, lets look at some of the options available to compensate for the limitations of the traditional education system.

Alternative Schools

Many parents are already catching on to the need for a new approach to education. For some, this means looking for schools that take an alternative approach to teaching and learning. Ron Miller, from the Alternative Education Resource Organization (AERO), has summarized the various different alternative approaches into six broad categories: "the transmission model, freedom-based learning, social constructivism, critical pedagogy, spiritual developmentalism, and integral or holistic education."[60]

The transmission model is commonly used in traditional educational institutions where information is transmitted from the adult to the student. It is important for parents who are adverse to such a model to recognize that there are alternative schools that continue to use this approach. For instance, while charter schools and bilingual schools are growing in popularity, many still follow the transmission model.

Another method, freedom-based learning, is most prevalent in democratic schools in which democratic principles are both a goal and a form of instruction. These communities also favor self-paced learning and flexible schedules (often convenient for traveling families).

The other alternative approaches Ron Miller outlines include educational institutions such as Montessori and Waldorf, as well as the educational philosophies of Jean Piaget, John Dewey and others. You can find a full list of alternative educational institutions around the world on the AERO site.

Homeschooling

One of the most well-known approaches outside of the formal educational system is that of homeschooling. The basic tenets of homeschooling involve the idea of recreating school at home. This, however, can incorporate many teaching methods, as well as teachers both inside and outside the home. And while it is common for homeschool parents to teach similar subjects and use some of the same structures as traditional schools, the homeschool environment allows for a more personalized and efficient approach.

As mentioned, most children can learn the basic skills and subjects taught in school without the endeavor consuming the majority of their young lives. My dear childhood friend told me about her homeschool years and I was surprised by the significantly small amount of time she actually spent on school. She would usually get her schoolwork done within three hours each day and then would spend the rest of the day playing outside with her siblings.

She also said that she hated waiting for all her other friends to get home from school. While she had the ability to complete her schooling at her convenience, we were all stuck in school for the better part of the day, no matter how quickly we learned the concepts being taught. The funny thing was, we were learning about the same things, I just spent a lot more time inside.

Homeschooling has gown over the past several decades, especially in the United States. According to Eric J. Isenberg, in 2007 in the U.S.,

> The number of homeschooled children [was] over 1 million, more than 2% of the total number of school children and roughly equal to the total in charter schools and voucher schools combined. There [was] approximately one

homeschooled child for every five children enrolled in private school.[32]

And just four years later, Peter Gray found that,

> The number of US children of school age (five to seventeen) who are homeschooled grew from about 850,000 in 1999 to an estimated two million or slightly more in 2011, or from about 1.7 percent to nearly 4 percent of the school-age population (p.227).[3]

There is also plenty of encouraging data that supports the superior nature of the homeschool approach. One particular study found that structured homeschooling students outperformed public school students by a dramatic margin.

> In 5 of 7 test areas, (word identification, phonic decoding, science, social science, humanities) structured homeschoolers were at least one grade level ahead of public schoolers.

> They were almost half a year ahead in math, and slightly, but not significantly, advanced in reading comprehension.

> In 5 of 7 areas, the differences were substantial, ranging from 1.32 grade levels for the math test to 4.2 grade levels for the word identification test.[33]

If you decide to take the homeschool route, the academics should not worry you. And as far as the prospects for college and employment go for the untraditionally educated, things look bright. Homeschooled, unschooled and world schooled students who have wanted to follow the university path have all found ways to do so – whether by taking the necessary exams, going to a community college and transferring or some other method. Plus, Peter Gray points out that,

> Homeschoolers graduate college at a higher rate than their peers– 66.7 percent compared to 57.5 percent. Not only that, but they earn higher grade-point averages than their schooled classmates along the way (p.76).[3]

And for those who choose not to go to college, apprenticeships are reemerging as a valid social script toward future employment (p.165).[17] It is becoming more and more apparent that college is not the only path toward a successful future. So, if your child has learned how to learn, trust their choices.

Unschooling

Whereas homeschooling still involves some of the structures of traditional schooling, unschooling completely rejects the school system and places full trust in the child to learn at their own pace, driven by their own interests.

The term "unschooling" was first coined by John Holt in the 1970s. He wasn't particularly happy with the term, however, preferring "Growing Without Schooling" (GWS) or "life" as better descriptive titles for his educational philosophy.

As we have already seen, children are constantly learning. We do not send them to kindergarten because they suddenly stop learning at five years old, but because we are accustomed to the educational systems that dictate such behavior. Holt realized that such an approach was actually stifling children's ability to learn, and argued that we should simply allow our children to learn from life as they are naturally programed to do. Eli Gerzon sums up the philosophy by explaining,

> It's essentially freedom or the confidence in free people's ability to become educated by utilizing the resources and guidance around them and inside of them. It is often described as "child driven learning", free of coercion and based on following one's own interests, not necessarily using any of the usual school resources. Still, one can go to classes and use textbooks while still calling oneself an unschooler as many unschoolers do.[34]

For both children and parents who are new to unschooling, there will likely be a period in which you will need to "deschool." This deschooling process comes as you readjust your mindset about what learning actually entails and how it happens – specifically, that it can occur outside a classroom without a schedule or neatly divided subjects.[35]

There is little data about the performance of unschoolers at this point, and what we do have is too limited to draw any final conclusions. For one, due to their (justifiable) aversion to standardized tests, unschoolers can be difficult to observe. One study, however, was able to compare unschoolers (referred to as unstructured homeschoolers in the study), homeschoolers (structured homeschoolers) and public school students.

According to the study, where homeschoolers performed above grade level, unschoolers performed below it – even after controlling for family income and maternal education. Unschoolers also performed slightly below public school students, but not by enough to rule out chance.

The researchers were quick to point out the limitations of their research, though, and advocated for more research to better understand unschooling. One explanation they gave for the lower test scores among unschoolers is that children who struggle to adapt to formal instruction are more likely to unschool, which could greatly affect the results of the study.[33]

I would add that since unschoolers do not follow the standardized teaching format, they are likely unprepared for the specific subject being tested. For now, we will have to rely on case studies of other unschoolers, which are actually very encouraging.[36]

World Schooling

Unlike homeschooling and unschooling, world schooling is a rather new educational philosophy and practice that has only begun to take form in the past decade or so. As such, it is still a bit hard to pin down. Some define it as a type of unschooling while others take a more structured approach – whether through homeschooling or immersion in local (foreign) schools. Moreover, among these different approaches, some choose to world school long-term, while others take a more short-term approach.

This difficulty to define world schooling does not, however, mean that there is not a unifying core tying all worldschoolers together. As I dove into the world schooling community, I discovered one great commonality: a deep appreciation for the world combined with a strong belief that children learn best by living in it.

This, in turn, calls for varying degrees of travel as part of a child's educational and life experiences. However, it is not travel alone that defines education through world schooling, but rather the mindset that comes with it. The drive to learn and the childlike curiosity about everything that surrounds us is what makes travel meaningful and converts the world into an unparalleled classroom.[34]

No doubt, world schooling is a marked effort to break out of the traditional education system. And what better way to revolutionize education than by pushing past the limits of how things are done and trying something thoroughly new? What better way to prepare our children for a globalized, inter-connected world than by taking them out into it to learn from it and the many wonderful people on this planet?

Why World Schooling?

Why choose world schooling over the other options available to you? In part, because you do not have to choose it over something else. Instead, world schooling is a tool available to enhance whatever educational approach you choose to take. As we will see in Section Two, there are many ways to world school.

However, before we get to all the nitty-gritty details of how to world school, let's answer just a few more important questions about why world schooling works in general. The first reason is that world schooling demands greater participation from the child. Whether you combine world schooling with homeschooling, unschooling, or some type of formal or alternative schooling, a child who travels cannot avoid the opportunities to learn.

Learning becomes a survival skill when you are far outside your comfort zone. And, for most of us, travel has a way of pushing us well beyond our comfort zones. The same is true for children. Providing a child with new cultures, countries, peoples and environments from which to learn is one of the best ways to jumpstart their natural instinct to learn. Even if you cannot see it happening, they are absorbing so much more than airplane rides or camping trips.

Because of this, world schooling works on an entirely different level because it not only demands and inspires greater participation from the child, but it also forces the parent to allow for more student-paced, self-directed learning.

Rather than lament the often hectic aspects of a traveling lifestyle, choose to embrace the experience. If you are finding it difficult to teach your children out of a textbook because you are traveling mountainous paths to live with indigenous peoples, throw the textbook out and learn from the experience! I learned more Spanish in the two weeks I spent in Guatemala than my previous two years in high school Spanish classes. I learned by conversing with the people and using my limited skills to ask for help to express what I really wanted to say. I learned what I wanted to learn because I needed to learn it based on real life circumstances.

Doesn't that sound just a little more practical, efficient and exciting than conjugating verbs in a textbook? And this does not just apply to language. It is much more inspiring to learn about ancient Roman architecture and Renaissance artists when you are in Italy than with your nose in a textbook. It is easier to understand the real world applications of marine biology when you are in the marina. And it is much easier for your children to want to learn about these things and direct their own learning when they are out there in the real world experiencing these things firsthand.

Sir Ken Robinson explained the profound need we have for this level of personalized, natural learning – not standardized textbooks, but natural learning from the context of real life:

> We have built our education systems on the model of fast food... everything is standardized... [instead of] customized to local circumstances. We have sold ourselves into a fast food model of education, and it's impoverishing our spirits and our energies as much as fast food is depleting our physical bodies...
>
> Human flourishing is not a mechanical process, it's an organic process. You cannot predict the outcome of human development. All you can do, like a farmer, is create the conditions under which they will begin to flourish. So when we look at reforming education and transforming it, it isn't like cloning a system... It's about customizing to your circumstances and personalizing education to the people you're actually teaching... It's about creating a movement in education in which people develop their own solutions, but with external support based on a personalized curriculum.[30]

While Sir Ken Robinson was not specifically talking about world schooling, his solution certainly fits the definition. World schooling allows for incredible levels of customization and personalized learning. By taking children out of the classroom and introducing them to the world, we are creating the conditions in which they can see, experience and learn. And by giving them these opportunities, they are more empowered than ever to direct their own learning.

Finally, world schooling stands out as an exceptional vehicle toward the end goals of education because of the incredibly positive impact it can have on the family. World schooling has the potential to free up your time so that you can focus on your family in unprecedented ways. The 9-to-5 routine that cuts into precious family time goes out the window when world schooling comes calling. If you are looking for a way to create and sustain a strong family while simultaneously giving your children the best caliber of education possible (mixed with a little adventure), then world schooling could be the perfect way to go.

Just keep in mind that no matter how you choose to educate your children, the important thing is that *you* define the purpose of education for both yourself and your family. From all my years researching education in college, combined with the years I spent teaching in a private school here in Mexico, the biggest factor of success I have been able to observe has always been family.

Recognize the power that you have to shape so much of your child's life. More importantly, recognize that *you* are the most influential person responsible for your child's education. Teachers, mentors, coaches, principals, professors and so many others will come and go, but nothing is so lasting and so powerful as that of family.

Hundreds of academic studies have confirmed and reconfirmed this. One study, conducted by the University of Michigan, found that "the single strongest predictor of better achievement scores and fewer behavioral problems was not time spent on homework, but rather the frequency and duration of family meals (p.113).[10] Family meals! Educational success is not rocket science. It just takes a lot of work on our part to create and sustain strong families.

If world schooling helps you achieve a stronger family, then it could be the right solution for you.

Just know that whether you send your children to a public school, a private school, a charter school, a democratic school, an international school, an alternative school, a vocational school, or you homeschool, unschool, or adopt some form of world schooling, the biggest influence on your child's education is *you*. If you value education and make those values a part of your home, most any form of education will produce positive results.

So, why keep reading this book? Why learn about world schooling if the most basic answer to all our educational woes is to foment strong family values? Certainly, the ideal is to have both a strong family *and* the best educational approach possible. In that light, world schooling is an attractive offer for both family and education.

You will also find that world schooling is flexible enough to adapt to the unique needs of each family. The "best approach" will not be the same for everyone, and what works for your family may look very different from the path that another family chooses to pursue. For that reason, the following chapters will introduce you to the many different ways families have chosen to world school so that you can find the approach that best fits your family.

In Section Two we will take a detailed look at the four main approaches worldschoolers use as they combine education and travel for a truly 21st-century education. One approach may stand out to you more than another, or you may find all the methods attractive and choose to create your own eclectic approach. The key is to find what works for your family. My hope is that you will use the rest of this book to gather ideas, form your own plan and then make the jump!

Section Two:
World Schooling

Chapter Four: The Settled Globetrotter

I can still picture the moment, sitting in my cousins' living room, all of us crowded around my aunt as she opened up an atlas. It was pure magic. I sat in wonder as she pointed out the places their family would visit that summer as they traveled to some distant country to help build schoolhouses and bathrooms in rural villages.

I was filled with an indescribable wonder as I watched my aunt and cousins pore over that magical map. I could not resist the urge to ask a million questions about the places and people, the land and animals, the culture and economy, the projects they would help carry out and so many other burning curiosities. I wanted to know everything!

Over the years, this same scene would repeat itself over and over again. Whether I was there or not, my cousins would research their planned destination and learn as much as they could. Upon their return, we would sit in the banana chairs in their living room and watch their family videos of adventures in the jungle, dances with the local children and the many sites they visited wherever they went. One of my favorite memories was watching home videos of kangaroos and bravely trying the vegemite my cousins brought home from their month-long visit to my aunt's family in Australia.

When my own high school graduation approached, my cousins began talking about their plans to travel to Guatemala that summer. I could resist no longer. During my sophomore year – as a representative of Guatemala in the Model United Nations High Commissioner for Refugees (UNHCR) – I had worked months on end studying the Guatemalan civil war and the human refugee crisis it had sparked among the country's indigenous people. My cousins would be in the very villages that had been affected by the crisis. I simply could not let this opportunity slip by... and so I asked if I could go with them. And they said yes!

That experience completely changed my life in more ways than I could ever hope to describe. Though it only lasted two weeks, I consider that trip one of the defining moments of my life. It changed my perspective of the world, my own culture, the meaning of development and strongly influenced where I chose to focus my college studies. Two weeks.

One of the mistakes that we make as we approach world schooling is to assume that it can only occur when we are traveling long-term. This could not be further from the truth. As we have established, world schooling goes beyond a certain lifestyle choice and – at its core – is a mindset. This mindset about how children learn and the role of travel in that learning process is what drives travel. How much you travel with your children matters much less than *why* you travel.

Do not make the mistake of thinking that two weeks out of the year is not enough. Yes, more would be ideal, but not all families are at the point where they either want or are able to travel for longer periods of time. That does not mean you cannot be a worldschooler. If anything, becoming a Settled Globetrotter can be the first step toward some of the other strategies that will be mentioned in the chapters to come. Whatever you choose, you can provide your children with incredible educational opportunities just by following the suggestions in this chapter.

One of the mistakes that we make as we approach world schooling is to assume that it can only occur when we are traveling long-term. This could not be further from the truth. As we have established, world schooling goes beyond a certain lifestyle choice and – at its core – is a mindset. This mindset about how children learn and the role of travel in that learning process is what drives travel. How much you travel with your children matters much less than *why* you travel.

hat does it mean to be a Settled Globetrotter? First and foremost, it does not require a specific schooling method beyond world schooling. Whether your children are homeschoolers, unschoolers or attend an alternative, private, charter or public school does not matter. The main idea is that your family spends most of their time in one location in your home or base country, but travels occasionally.

Now, the definition of "occasionally" may differ greatly from one Settled Globetrotter family to the next. For the purposes of this book, however, we will consider travel durations from one day to one year to fall under this first category. Families that are traveling a full year may adopt other strategies discussed later on, but for the most part, the main thing Settled Globetrotters have in common is that they have a home base from which they operate and spend the majority of their life.

This strategy works well for families that do not have a location independent source of income or who have familial obligations that do not allow them to travel long term. It is also great for those of us who like a little stability, want to participate in an established community, or who want to practice the principles of homesteading and raising your own food.

Furthermore, it is a great starting off point for those considering a more extreme world schooling lifestyle. Many of the families that I interviewed who are now living full time overseas began with a short-term trip to a location that interested the whole family, just to test the waters before fully committing. Here are a couple of their stories:

Brandon Pearce:

> It started back when we were living in Salt Lake, [Utah]. We had always wanted to travel. Jen and I had both been internationally before we had kids and a little bit together without the kids, but we wanted to take the kids to have a broader experience. But it was more of a dream of a "someday we'll do it" kind of a thing. We were just planning to go down the regular path of go to school, have a regular career and then eventually maybe something like that will happen.

> There were a few things that led up to the decision to world school. Part of it was related to our financial situation because I was studying to become a computer programmer and I was also teaching piano lessons on the side. Around that time, my father-in-law lost his job at a high-tech company and I just realized that there's no such thing as job security when you work for somebody else.

So, I started to look for ways to provide for my family... that I would have a lot more control over than working for somebody else. Around that time, I had also been working on a little application to help me manage my piano students and keep track of their billing and scheduling. I decided to turn that into a business and start selling it as a subscription service. I worked hours and hours and hours on that thing and it slowly, slowly grew. After a couple years, it got to the point where I realized that there might actually be some potential here to completely support my family. So, I quit my programming job which I had at that point and just continued to build up the business.

It was around this time that I encountered some books like "The Power of Less" by Leo Babauta – a fantastic book about minimalism and living with less. [This helped me realize] that the whole consumeristic culture that I was surrounded by was something that just didn't appeal to me and I felt like I was stagnating in my personal growth.

This is what really led us into the world schooling journey because I just felt like I could see my future and the trajectory that my life was on: I would do what everyone around me was doing, which was working harder and harder, driving my kids to so many classes, getting a bigger house, a nicer car and a lot more stuff. But I knew deep down that it wouldn't make me any more fulfilled or happy than I already was.

I wanted something different. I wanted a broader experience. So, "The Power of Less" helped me a lot with being able to shed some of the stuff that I had and clearing out the clutter from my life – [the] physical stuff and other stuff. It was about realizing what I didn't need and identifying the essential things in my life and eliminating the rest...

It came to a point where I realized, "Wait a minute, I'm here feeling kind of stagnate, I want to give my kids a more international experience, but I'm actually in a place now where I can do that. I'm not working at a full-time job, I could do this work I'm doing from anywhere." And it just kind of clicked with me, "Well, why don't we do this? I could pursue this lifestyle."

Something else happened around this time that really pushed us out the door and that was that my wife's mother got cancer at 50 and passed away. That was a really emotionally difficult time for all of us, obviously. And it really drove home to me and to all of us that life is short and I don't want to be working and going through the motions of life only to finally enjoy it once I hit retirement. I want to find greater purpose and meaning and joy and fulfillment in life right now and I do not want to delay that. And that really got us into gear, figuring out how to do this and making it work.

Our first jump into it was a six-week trip to Panama that we took just to test the waters. And it was so much more than we ever imagined. When we went, we were still planning on sending our kids to school (they were in pre-school at the time). We kind of toyed with the idea of homeschooling, but it sounded too hard and we thought, "We don't really want to do that." But we met a family in Panama that was homeschooling and that kind of just inspired us to realize that maybe we can do this.

The six weeks in Panama was so bonding as a family. We grew so much closer together than we'd ever been because we were together 24/7. We wondered if we would drive each other crazy, but we didn't and it just worked out great and we came back and we realized that we wanted to do this more and so that's when we sold our house, got rid of all our stuff and made a more permanent move the following year to Costa Rica.[4]

Lainie Liberti

In 2008, when the economy crashed, I owned a business. I had worked in marketing and branding and advertising for almost 18-19 years and the last eight years I had my own agency – a small design firm that focused on branding. When the economy crashed, I watched my bread and butter clients start going away and I knew that I was going to have to close my agency.

Now, a lot of things led up to that moment of decision. The biggest influence was my son telling me constantly, "Mom, you never spend any time with me. You're always working." That was very hurtful and, even though I knew it was true, being a single parent I believed I was doing everything I had to do and I believed that I had no other choice or option. But when the economy crashed, I knew that I would be forced to make changes in my life.

So, with my son telling me these things, I started to feel this inspiration inside of me. It was this sort of burst of energy around my heart that just kept growing and growing and growing and growing. I call it inspiration. And every time I tapped into feeling that, it would say, "Go have an adventure! Go travel!"

One night, we were sitting in the office and I remember looking at my son and I said, "Sweetie, let's get rid of everything!" I was so afraid to tell him that we had to make a change in our lives. I was so afraid that he would be afraid of making a change or that it would be a scary thing for him. And I just looked at him and said, "Honey, let's go have an adventure."

And I started to tell him about this inspiration I was feeling. We did a search online and looked at all these tropical places and Costa Rica came up and Mexico and all these other places and we just looked at pictures and I said, "Let's just go have an adventure!" And he said, "Oh yeah, I'm in! Let's do it!"

[I had been] so scared that he wasn't going to do it, that he wouldn't be open to it, but that was that moment. It was the most incredible, life-changing moment besides giving birth to him. That was it. It was a big moment. I'll never forget how it felt and the impact and the feeling that I had around my heart – that embodiment of inspiration and knowing that I never knew that I had, but it was there, driving me. Then, once he was on board, I knew that we were unstoppable.

Of course, at that time I knew it was a one year adventure that we had planned. When you live a conventional life, two weeks seems like a long time. One year was like, "That's forever!" And we never believed in that moment that it would be indefinite. But now we're sitting here in Greece and it's eight years later. I never knew that [would happen]. If you would have told me then that that was going to be our reality, I would have laughed. But this all started with all of these things lining up and then that internal knowing.

Before we started traveling, my son had been in a Montessori school up until the end of second grade and then he was in a traditional school in third and fourth grade. I knew when we started traveling that we were supposed to be gone for only one year. I also knew that he was going to learn so much more than he would in fifth grade by traveling.

So, I knew that instinctively with every cell in my being that this was going to be much more of an education. He wouldn't have missed anything. Fifth grade had nothing on a year of travel. I knew that. But I always had that belief that he'd always go back to being enrolled in school once we got back.

When we were about eight months into our travels, however, my son and I decided together that there was really no reason for us to go back. We were enjoying what we were doing.[29]

From Lainie and Brandon's stories, it is easy to see how a short-term trip can become a full-time travel and world schooling lifestyle. Short-term travel can also be a great solution for those who want to travel full-time, but are still working on developing a source of location independent income and do not want to put off traveling any longer. Later on, we will also see examples of families who, after extensive travel, have chosen to become Settled *Expatriate* Globetrotters, meaning that they have set up a permanent home base in a foreign country from which they will travel on occasion.

However, for many families who wish to world school without ever permanently leaving their home country, this first approach to world schooling can be the method of choice from the outset. For those of us who do not plan on selling all our belongings and taking off on an indefinite global adventure, being a Settled Globetrotter is not about dipping your toe in to see if you want to commit to more, it is about creating a long-term world schooling mindset from home, with as much travel as possible.

I talk to people all of the time who want to travel and incorporate world schooling into their family culture, but do not want the nomadic lifestyle that seems to inevitably come with it. Take, for example, the mother of small children whose husband has a location *dependent* career that is doing incredible things for the less fortunate in their community. Or, the couple that also values homesteading and wants to teach their children to raise their own food. Or, the father who traveled non-stop when he was young and wants his children to enjoy the benefits of travel as well, without sacrificing the stability and childhood friendships he was unable to experience.

For these families, world schooling would seem to be an impossibility –but it is not! Approaching world schooling as a Settled Globetrotter is a perfectly valid way of becoming a worldschooler. Remember, world schooling is not just about travel but also the global mindset and the value you place on travel and connecting to other people, places and cultures.

In her book, "Give Your Child the World: Raising Globally Minded Kids One Book at a Time"[37], Jamie C. Martin outlines some amazing strategies that Settled Globetrotters can use to incorporate a world schooling mindset into their daily lives. While I recommend you actually read her book, here is a summary of the main strategies she suggests, with my own observations thrown in:

Books: Books are a secret travel portal that can transport a child anywhere in the world. Fill your homes with books about different countries, peoples, foods, cultures, languages, environments and all the other amazing things around our incredible planet. Jamie Martin suggests giving book talks to your children to pique their interest. Present the book and then let them decide what they want to read. She also provides a great list of books about every area of the world and for every age.

Movies: Teach your children to be more than just passive movie watchers. Encourage them to analyze movies and pick up on the historical and cultural backgrounds in which the stories take place. Then, use whatever you have watched as a springboard for further learning. Did you just watch a movie that takes place in China? Go to the library and find a good book or go online and look up what you can about Chinese culture, history, art, etc. Was it a story from Chinese history? Look up the real story. Did the characters use a form of martial arts? Research that. A movie can be much more than a form of entertainment!

YouTube Videos: The amount of content available on the World Wide Web these days is truly staggering. You can easily take a child's interest in any topic and look it up and find hundreds of videos about it online. While I think we are all pretty familiar with YouTube, just take this as a friendly reminder to use it for educational purposes.

Music: Music is such an interesting reflection of culture that you can easily bring into your home. You can go from the mountainous regions of Bolivia to the desert sands of Saudi Arabia within minutes by simply listening to music from those regions. As with movies, you can turn music into a deeper educational experience by encouraging your children to investigate more about the underlying musical traditions across the world.

Food: Trying new foods is one of the great draws of travel; but you do not necessarily have to travel to try the cuisines of the world. Look for international restaurants near your home and make a point of taking your family out for an international food night on a regular basis. Not a fan of eating out? Invite your children into the kitchen and have them look up recipes from around the world that they can then help you prepare and eat. Have them write a review of the meal to practice their writing skills or, if they are learning another language, have them find a dish from a country where that language is spoken and have them write the recipe up in the foreign language.

Dress: Children love a chance to dress up. Expand their imaginations and introduce them to the traditional dress of cultures all over the world. While it is not my specialty, if you are teaching your kids to sew, you could have them learn to sew a piece of clothing worn in a different country. Get creative. Have a fashion show. Learn the dances that so often accompany traditional dresses. Learn the history. Do reports. Have fun!

Travel Preparation: Before traveling to another country, set aside some time to research the country's history to give context to the places and people you will meet along the way. During college, I conducted oral history interviews with the oldest members of several rural communities in Mexico. Even though I was right there, in the village with the people, I did not understand half the things they were talking about.

It wasn't until I took a class on the history of Mexico upon my return to university that those interviews even made sense. In fact, after I understood the context, I went back and listened to the interviews once more and they were beyond fascinating! The same rule applies to learning about the wildlife, nature, economy, culture, and a thousand other topics you could research before going to your destination of choice.

Holidays: Feeling festive? Have your children research the different holidays celebrated around the world and then make plans to do a little celebrating of your own. There are enough holidays celebrated in every country of the world that you could plan a celebration every week. This would be a great way to include the food and dress of a country into your learning adventures as well.

The Arts: Discover the different forms of art practiced all across the globe. Read the works of great poets in their native tongue (for language learners), learn about the great works of art, or go see a show from a traveling group of cultural performers. Go to a museum and take advantage of the traveling exhibits that feature some of the great works. Invite your children to write their own poems or create their own pieces of art based on the different styles you have researched. The options are plentiful.

Maps/Globes: The home of any worldschooler should be sure to have maps, atlases, and globes out in the open, or readily available for use. My parents placed two large maps on our wall, one of the U.S. and the other of the world. We would put little pins in all the places we had visited. We also had a globe that my brothers and sisters and I would play with by spinning it and landing our fingers on a random spot to determine where we were going to travel one day.

You can, of course, use these tools in a much more directed way for geography lessons and more, but just having them around the house is a great way to inspire your child's curiosity about the world.

Humanitarian Efforts: One of the best ways to help your children feel connected to the world and positive about their ability to make an impact for good in it is to give them opportunities to serve. I still remember the clothing drive my fourth grade teachers helped us organize throughout our elementary school to help the victims of a hurricane in Honduras. And I have happy memories of spending family reunions assembling baby receiving kits and educational bags for children in Africa.

You can, of course, take this one step further and take your family on one of the many humanitarian expeditions to all the corners of the earth. There are many phenomenal humanitarian organizations that use the money from their travel packages to fund the building of schools, hospitals, bathrooms, and water treatment programs, or finance their efforts to stop child trafficking, support refugees or help the less-advantaged start small businesses. Find an organization with a cause that you and your children believe in and then find a way to help both at home and abroad.

Pen Pals: Connect your child with another child in a different part of the world. Have them send letters to practice their writing skills or organize a video chat to improve language abilities. Encourage your child to learn about their pen pal's country, history, culture, economy, geography, etc. Have them learn as much as they can from their pen pal, but also invite them to do their own research to be more informed.

Exchange Students and World Travelers: Welcome exchange students into your home. Even if you are not spending all of your time traveling the world, that does not mean the world cannot come to you! Aren't quite ready to share your home full time? Invite world travelers into your home. Reach out to the refugee and immigrant communities or invite a friend who has traveled to other countries to come share pictures and stories.

Visit Immigrant Communities: Go beyond the walls of your home and take your kids to visit a community with a different cultural background from your own. Find events taking place and ask if it would be alright for you and your children to join in. Many communities will put on festivals where they recreate the dances, food, and even the street markets typical in their home countries. For some families, purposefully choosing to live in a more ethnically and racially diverse neighborhood may be the perfect learning experience.

Country Reports and Passport Packages: Have your children write up and present reports about a country of their choice. They can research everything from imports and exports to religion and history to current events and more. If you want a more structured approach, Jamie Martin suggests the Little Passports packages that arrive each month, full of activities to learn more about one country.

Site-See at Home: There are plenty of places you can visit within a small distance from your home. Go on traveling adventures with your children to discover the plants and animals in your area, investigate more about the environment, visit museums and historical sites, learn about different religions in your area, ask for a tour of a local business, plan a field trip to the mayor's office, etc.

––––––

While there are many, many ways to learn about the world from home, a true world schooler will still look for opportunities to actually travel whenever they can. These travel opportunities can take many shapes and forms – from taking a week-long road trip across the country to getting on a plane and traveling to the other side of the world for six months. Here are just a few ideas to get you started:

Summers Abroad: If you are tied to a school schedule, be sure to take advantage of the summer season as much as you can. Pick a country, city, or any number of countries where you can travel and spend your summer months. If you do some sort of homeschool and have a relatively flexible or location independent source of income, then you can take a Spring or Winter Abroad, or whatever period of time works best for your family.

Sabbatical or Gap Years: Many families have the fortune of taking off a full year of work through either a sabbatical or a gap year. If you are planning on doing this, I would suggest you take a look at the rest of the chapters in this section to get ideas on how to approach long-term education on the road. While you will be coming home at some point, you will want to have a vision and a plan for handling your child's education while you are gone. Here are a couple of insightful nuggets from Maya Frost for now:

> Wise parents on sabbatical choose to focus on their children's development rather than on their education. This is true for kids of all ages but especially for those under ten. Parents need to emphasize exposure to new cultures and languages (and happy times spent with the family) rather than academic rigor. Going on a sabbatical is a wonderful opportunity to evolve the brain… in all kinds of ways, but enrolling a kid in a highly competitive school abroad so he won't "fall behind" misses the point entirely (p.248).

> If you're considering taking a family sabbatical, talk to those who've actually been on one instead of those who have concerns about the idea. Even better, find an enlightened

educator who has spent time abroad. This will ease your mind and pave the way for conversations with teachers and colleagues (p.255).[27]

However long you travel, and no matter how you choose to educate your children while on the road, once you are home, be sure to create opportunities to reflect on and continue to learn from your trip.

Study Abroad: Studying abroad will provide your children with numerous benefits as they travel alone to a new country during the formative years of high school. Many high schools offer foreign exchange and study abroad programs. If you homeschool or your high school does not offer a program, Rotary International is a fantastic organization to work with. In her book, "The New Global Student", Maya Frost outlines all the nitty gritty details for making the most of a study abroad experience. If you are interested in taking this route, I would highly recommend you read her book. As she puts it,

> The innovative leaders of the future—those who will be snagging those creative class jobs (or making their own) all over the planet—aren't simply meeting in the lobby for their daily scheduled bus tour. Instead, they're embracing the bold-school approach to study abroad: go solo, go long, and go deep (p.182).[27]

Travel!: For many Settled Globetrotters, opportunities to travel may present themselves at inconvenient times or in unconventional ways. Worldschoolers will want to take advantage of these opportunities whenever they can. Doing so successfully will often depend on having the right game plan ready to handle the challenges and objections you will face. Traveling while tied to the schedules and responsibilities of a more established lifestyle that tends to gravitate toward predictability does not have to conflict with being a worldschooler.

For example, if your child is studying in a traditional school with the typical fall to spring schedule, it may seem impossible or even irresponsible to take your child out of school to go travel the world for weeks or even months at a time. I know I used to feel this way as a teacher – as if the parents were compromising their child's education in exchange for leisure. (Don't worry, I have come a long way since then.) However, I am 100% positive I would have wholeheartedly supported my students' travel if the parents had come to me with the kind of plan Jennifer Miller suggests in one of her masterful articles. I am sharing part of that article here with her permission:

If you approach your school with a two-fold educational plan, what your child will learn and how your child will "keep up," you will be very likely to be met with enthusiasm and encouragement from the educational establishment. Highlight the educational benefits and focus on curricular subjects:

- History: Museums, historical sites, battlefields etc. that you plan to visit.
- Geography: Come armed with maps and discuss the mountains you'll climb, the oceans you'll sail or swim, and the cultural implications of time in the world for your child.
- Language Arts: Create a book list for your teacher from which your child will choose to read two or three (this can easily be done with an Amazon topical search).
- Science: Historical sites are full of science, so are ecological tours and adventures. Marine biology and SCUBA lessons go hand in hand. Visit a baboon sanctuary in Belize or tour a mine in Arizona.
- You get the idea; demonstrate that there is educational benefit to the trip for your child and demonstrate that you intend to maximize it. Work with the teacher and develop a plan for your child to maintain his current work.

There are a few things that you can do that will benefit the entire class your child belongs to, perhaps the entire school. Here are a few ideas:

- Turn your journey into a virtual field trip
- Allow your child to communicate with the class from abroad
- Create video-logues for his classmates
- Send postcards
- Take a Flat Stanley
- Create daily news reports for the class
- Start a blog
- Take in a big map and let the kids in the class follow your route

- Skype from somewhere far flung during school hours
- Have the class create a scavenger hunt for your child to complete on the journey & bring the items home
- If you want to really be fabulous, create a book list, find activities online that relate, and compile a whole file that the teacher can easily turn into a "Unit Study" or a party when you return from the place you're going for the whole class.

If you want to take your child out of school for some alternative learning, then you're going to need to be ready to demonstrate what the child has learned in a way that is meaningful to the school. Here's the Key:

- Craft a pitch
- Demonstrate that your child will be learning
- Quantify the results
- Bonus points if you can benefit the whole class [38]

While it may not seem like Settled Globetrotters get the whole world schooling experience, the truth is that they can easily reach the same end goals for their child's education as someone traveling long-term. If you have the right mindset and make the effort to travel when you can, world schooling as Settled Globetrotters will be a rewarding and enjoyable educational approach for your whole family.

Chapter Five: The Unconventional Traditionalist

"Hola! Cómo están?" I heard a little voice say as I boarded my flight home from Guatemala. I looked around the plane in search of the child who had said hello, sure he was a native speaker. To my surprise, my eyes landed on the face of a towheaded four-year-old boy peeking over the seat in front of me. "Hola!" I replied, to which the little boy responded with a long stream of native Spanish my two years of high school Spanish could barely understand.

My cousins and I were blown away. We expressed our amazement to the boy's mother and asked how her son had learned to speak like a native Guatemalan by the age of four. She explained that every summer she would travel to Guatemala to enjoy the sites and do a bit of work so that she could enroll her son in a preschool in the area. He was totally surrounded by Spanish and the Spanish culture during that time and – as the little sponge that children are – he had just soaked it all up. Amazing.

This was my first encounter with an Unconventional Traditionalist. I was impressed with her ingenuity, to say the least. Unconventional Traditionalists are the parents who know how to use traditional systems in unconventional ways to achieve unconventional ends. For all the limitations of the traditional school system, Unconventional Traditionalists know that if they combine travel with local schools overseas, they can give their children a unique educational and social experience. It is, in a sense, a way to use the system to beat the system.

Not all Unconventional Traditionalists use this particular world schooling approach for the same reasons. And though it may or may not appeal to you right away, a closer look could reveal convincing reasons to give this strategy a try. Here are just a few of the reasons Unconventional Traditionalists use this particular approach:

Children's Opportunities to Socialize

There may come a point in your travels when you or your children would like more opportunities to socialize with other children and families. As Maya Frost explains, "The nuclear family is a fine thing as a home base for raising children, but for healthy development, children need to explore beyond it, even when they are little (p.226)."[27] This can often be difficult to achieve while on the road 24/7. Placing your children in a local school system – even if for a short period of time – may be the perfect break from such a parent-centric life and allow children to expand beyond the nuclear family and establish friendships.

In an article he wrote about his family's world school experience, Cliff Hsia explained the benefits of this approach that his daughters enjoyed while traveling the world.

> They learn more. Rather than being confined to one school at home with the same setting, the same playground and the same friends, they are exposed to so much more when they travel and study abroad. They play with kids of different social, cultural, and economic backgrounds, they hear and speak different languages, they see and experience different lifestyles, and they learn that there are many ways to learn about themselves and the world they live in. They also develop the intangibles of fearlessness, empathy, and adaptability by being in so many different places with different people.

> They have fun. The kids learn about different cultures and play in different environments. They get to go on field trips to local parks, zoos, museums, swimming pools, and beaches. And the best part about it is that they get to do these fun activities with their friends.[39]

Parental Free-Time

Another great reason to use the Unconventional Traditionalist's strategy is that it frees up parents' time and demands slower-paced travel. Cliff Hsia said it best:

> We find balance with our kids in school. My wife and I enjoy our time with our kids, but not all of our time, especially when we're traveling. Having the kids in school allows us to do some stress-free sightseeing, go for longer walks, exercise, and rest. World schooling our kids gives us balance to travel for longer periods of time with the peace of mind that our kids are engaged while we are in new places.
>
> World schooling our kids makes our family travel meaningful. Sightseeing, shopping, and eating together are great activities in new countries. But what makes the experience of traveling together special is that our kids have been fully engaged and benefited from traveling in their own ways through school.[39]

The other benefit of this approach is that you do need to put down roots, at least for a little while, in order for it to work. Several of the families I interviewed mentioned settling down for one month, six months and even nine months at a time to rest from the frenetic pace of perpetual travel and allow their children (and themselves) the chance to catch their breath and build deeper relationships with the people in the surrounding community.

And the great thing is that you do not have to move back home to get this kind of stability and rest from the constant wear of travel. You can still be world schooling, even if you have put down roots for a while. Daniel Prince and his family traveled non-stop for two and a half years after leaving their life and job in Singapore. Now, however, they have decided to slow down and enroll their children in a school near the home they are renting in France. He recounts their experience of adjusting to this new pace of life:

> For the kids to start school was a big change because they hadn't done that for many years. They were kind of nervous, like you and I would be starting a job and walking into an office on the first day.
>
> But those nerves were shattered within a week. They were having sleepovers with their French friends and it was just

instant. It was incredible. And 90% of that is because of the community that we moved into. And [I imagine] if we had moved into a school in Spain, Mexico, Germany, wherever, it would be similar.

And we're still world schooling. This isn't our native tongue, this isn't our native home, we're here, we're going to make new friends, we're going to integrate into the culture, we're going to integrate into the society and make friends with the people around us.[5]

While you may use a different world schooling approach at other times, becoming an Unconventional Traditionalist may provide you, your children, and your family some needed rest and relief while preparing for more fast-paced travel in the future. Or, you may find that you simply enjoy this slower pace and adopt it long-term, traveling to a new country maybe only once or twice a year as you fully take in the culture and people of your chosen location.

Cliff Hsia had this to say about the slower-paced travel that the Unconventional Traditionalist approach allows:

Putting our kids in local schools allowed us to slow our travel down. We were able to just pick a spot and stay put for a while and just be there and soak everything in and integrate ourselves into whatever community we were in. We could make friends because there were parents sending their kids to schools so we were able to meet other people through that network.[40]

Language

One of the most compelling reasons to become an Unconventional Traditionalist (at least from my perspective) is to gain the full benefits of immersion in order to dominate a foreign language. Children have a tremendous capacity to learn new languages, and immersion is probably THE most effective way for anyone to learn a language. You could not ask for a more perfect age or a better place for learning than the situation of immersing children in foreign language environments.

Local schools in the country where your target language is spoken make for great foreign language environments. Not only are classes taught in the language, but your children's friends will speak that language all day long throughout their playtime and as they establish deeper friendships. Your children will have to learn to read, write, speak and listen by virtue of necessity because they'll be surrounded by it constantly.

It may sound a little cruel to simply throw your children into such a situation, and it is certainly not for everyone, but it is not as impossible a situation as it sounds. This is especially true the younger your children are. When my husband and I first got engaged, one of my biggest questions was how we would teach our children both his native Spanish and my native English. I went to work researching as much as I could and found hundreds of studies confirming the same thing: children are wired to learn languages.

In fact, some studies have found that a baby can distinguish between different languages almost from the moment he or she is born (and most studies agree that this is true at least as early as six months of age). Furthermore, most agree that the younger a child learns a new language, the easier it will be for them to acquire a native accent.

Now that my son is beginning to speak in both languages, I get a lot of questions about this. When I explain all the research, people are always so surprised by a child's ability to learn. But we cannot make the same mistake. We cannot underestimate our children's ability to learn. If language is a priority for your family, take advantage of this innate ability to learn new languages while your children are young and provide them with the best environments to do so.

This is what the Prince family did. After years of constant travel, they sat down and had a discussion about what it was they actually wanted their children's education to achieve (think Chapter One) and what they decided led them to change their entire world schooling strategy. Here's their story:

When we first started traveling, we didn't have a set structure, which was nice. We have met people who homeschool and have that set structure, and we've met people who world school wherever they go and that kind of sets the tone for them. Or, their child will pick a subject and they'll dive deep into the particular subject that the child has shown interest in in the first place. We've just winged it along the way really.

Our focus now is the language, for sure, because Claire and I agreed that if we could give any one thing to our children and for our children to graduate with… if we had the option to take a box – one box, whether it's math, science, etc. – and we could triple A star plus all the way through to a degree or something, we both agreed that it would be language. So, if we came to that decision, then we needed to get somewhere and learn that language.

The language will not be learned in a classroom in England, for example. Very, very, very few people who go through that education are going to come out at the end of it at the age of 15, fluent in French or Spanish or German, or whatever it is they're studying. Whereas, if we decide to come to France and spend just nine months – one school year here, and after that school year, for whatever reason, we might want to move on – those nine months in French schools would have given them such a base and they will likely even be fluent.

So, that was the driving force. Coming to that realization that that was what we really wanted for our kids, that was what drove us. What made us choose France was that we had been here a couple times already and the kids had shown a real love for the country and the culture and a real interest in the language, so we asked the kids, "If we're going to go somewhere and learn a new language, where do you want to go?" And the two oldest ones who, at that point, were ten and eight, both picked France immediately. So we said, "Okay, let's start looking into that!"

Now that we are here and enjoying the experience, I feel as though we're on a holding pattern to see how it pans out here. I have a sneaking suspicion that coming in towards the end of the school year everybody is going to be really happy and they will want to stay here for another year and carry on and improve on their French. If, for some reason, it wasn't working out, then we'd love to look into the possibility of a different country and a different language.

It seems to us that, if we were to move to England, find a house and settle down, that's too easy. We're not pushing ourselves forward. There's loads to be achieved by living just a little bit differently and pushing that envelope and challenging yourselves.[5]

Stories like this one from the Prince family begin to help us understand the versatility of world schooling as a mindset. Any resource, even traditional schools, can become a tool to achieve a greater end, from language to community. And not every Unconventional Traditionalist uses the same strategy. Cliff Hsia and his family used a system that could be a great strategy for families still looking to move on a more regular basis. He explained his strategy to me in an interview:

Basically, we started traveling as soon as we had our second child. As a family of four, our first trip was to Nicaragua when our second daughter was six months and our oldest was about three years old. From there, one country led to another. We ended up going to four countries in South America. After that trip, I was working remotely at the time and we just got the travel bug and wanted to do more and more of it with out kids and integrate it into our lifestyle. I would do business trips domestically or sometimes we'd go and visit the kids' grandparents in China (my wife is from China).

But then, we really wanted to make it part of our lifestyle, especially while the kids were young and we had the freedom to take them wherever we chose. So, we started out with a month in Guatemala and then we did a month in Taiwan, then three months in China. So that was about a half year. Then we came back to the states and I did some work for about half a year and then my wife and I decided to take a gap year. The kids were about six and three at the time and we ended up going to about ten countries in ten months.

Over those last two or three years of extensive travel, we put our kids in schools outside of the United States in five countries: Guatemala for one month, Taiwan for one month, China for a total of about four months, Phuket, Thailand for three months and the last one was Barcelona, Spain for about a month. So, in total they've had their study abroad year spread out over a period of about two years.

They are seven and four now and they are back in their respective schools. One is in pre-school and the other is in second grade here in the Bay Area. But they've already had those different experiences, especially before they really started in the school system here in the United States. We're just really grateful and fortunate that we've had that experience with them. I think it has definitely shaped who they are.

In terms of being able to learn the language, we speak Chinese at home so in Taiwan and China they were able to reinforce their language. I think their language skills in Chinese got a lot better being in that type of immersive environment. For Spanish, in both instances in Spain and Guatemala they were in bilingual/trilingual environments where English was one of the languages. They did pick it up a little bit; certainly a lot faster than my wife and I would, but because we weren't there for that long (we were only one month in each of those countries) it didn't really stick.

And then Thailand, as well, they were there for three months. My oldest one was in first grade there and she had one of her classes as a Thai class. This was interesting because she was learning how to speak and write Thai — which just blew me away. She ended up learning how to sing the national anthem in Thai. We were at the airport one time and she was reading the signs, or letters in Thai and some Thai person nearby us was, just like me, blown away.

I couldn't really comprehend that she actually knew what she was seeing because they are all squiggly lines for me, but it's just incredible to actually see how easy it is for kids to acquire languages, especially when they're immersed in them and in that environment. That was one of the reasons I wanted to take them abroad and show them some different cultures, but also acquire an affinity for language learning.

Our expectations of what our children would learn by going abroad kind of evolved over time. We just took it one trip at a time. At first it was just to spend time together and be on vacations and bond as a family in different environments. Just having fun doing it while traveling. As our kids got older, they have their own opinions and need to be occupied. They can't just be towed around different countries.

One of the ways we thought about getting them engaged in their travels was actually having them be in the local schools. After doing a lot of sight seeing in different places all around the world and going to different shopping malls and parks, those kind of activities all become a blur and can kind of get old after a while, even if you're doing them in different places around the world. So, for our kids, we wanted to keep them engaged in the travel and personalize the experience for them so that they had something that was unique to their experience while traveling.

It was never planned that we were going to send our kids to school, we just kind of fell upon it. In Guatemala, we had a friend who was a teacher at a Montessori pre-school. They were just starting their semester the day after we had dinner with their family and I asked her if we could check it out and see if we could just earn our keep while we were in Guatemala for the four weeks that we were there. Within half an hour of speaking to the teacher and the principal and telling them our situation and agreeing to pay the monthly fee, we had our kids in there that afternoon.

It was an easy model that we were able to replicate wherever we went. In Taiwan we did the same thing. We were essentially located in Taipei and then we just walked around where we were living and found some different pre-schools (because they were both pre-school age at the time). We told them our situation and said we would only be there short-term and then we just asked them to see if we could put them in the school to have that learning experience while we were there.

For the most part, every school that we talked to was receptive of it. No matter what country we were in, they were open to allowing short-term students to go into their classroom – especially if it was a multilingual environment. I think they're used to that, having expats come and go, whether it be for a year or less.

We just did that everywhere we went. We did that in China, Thailand and Barcelona. We never even called in advance. We just arrived and went to a school in the area and asked if we could have our girls in the school and it worked out almost every single time.[40]

From these two experiences, it is easy to see the many benefits of placing your child in local schools. If you do not have the time or desire to place your children in local schools, it is good to know that this is not the only way for a child to learn another language. While living in Chile, I would spend an hour each morning studying the language and then spend the rest of the day out in the streets and in people's homes having conversations and using my Spanish non-stop.

If I found that I didn't know how to say something during the day, I would jot it down in a notebook and then look it up during my hour of language study the next day. If your child is at an age where they can practice this type of strategy on their own, without a school, then they may not need a school to gain language proficiency.

Superior Resources

There are also times where attending a formal educational institution makes sense for the world schooling family simply because a particular school offers the kind of resources that cannot be found on the road. It may also be the case that you find a school that uses superior teaching techniques and methods that you feel would benefit your child.

Theodora, from Escape Artistes, explained her reasons for settling down with her son at two different times during their travels and enrolling in local schools. The first and most important reason for doing so is that her son wanted to go to a school. This is something that, as parents, we must be very sensitive to. Children will learn best when they are involved in the process and feel they have a choice about where and how they study. If they choose to go to a formal school, they will be much better off than if that was simply something they did out of convention, or if they were forced to be homeschooled or unschooled. Choice matters.

The first time Theodora enrolled her son Zac in a formal school was in China, where he was able to greatly improve his Chinese, but also his math skills. Zac transitioned from unschooling to attending a 3000-child high school in China. She explains that her son was constantly challenged, and his math skills improved tremendously since Chinese seventh graders cover math most Western educational institutions do not touch until much later on.[41]

After some more traveling, they decided to settle down on a more permanent basis in Bali so that Zac could attend an international high school. Theodora explains that one of the main reasons they decided to do this is because, "Science, especially hard science, the area he's most interested in, is insanely hard to do well without the resources of a fixed abode or, frankly, a school... [Also,] creative arts are difficult to do well on the road. A lot of resources – like lasers and 3D printers for design & technology, or potter's wheels – are the sort of kit that, generally, only institutions invest in."[42]

While the experience also provided her son with a chance to establish friendships and have his own personal space, school in this case provided Zac with resources and learning opportunities that would not be available to someone who was traveling on a regular basis without a formal school. Theodora and Zac are committed to staying in one spot for the entire high school period to ensure that Zac has the academics necessary for college entry. So far, they have been in Bali for three years. A great way to settle down without going back to your home country.

I find this strategy particularly fascinating and would be interested in going to a place like Finland where the educational system is so much more innovative and advanced just to experience their schools. You could design your travel plans around the greatest educational systems in the world and try each one out until you find a good fit. You could take the best from each part of the world, learning math in China and art in Europe, making the system serve your needs wherever you go, rather than dealing with whatever your local public schools have to offer back at home.

Actively seeking out the best schools and learning opportunities is what makes the Unconventional Traditionalist's use of formal educational institutions so different from the typically passive approach. While you may be wary of schools, do not write them off altogether until you consider how you can use formal schools across the globe to serve your children's educational end goals.

Chapter Six: The Structured Adventurer

For the majority of families who travel with school-aged children, the most common and practical way to approach education is through some form of homeschooling. Travel requires flexibility in more areas than one, and education is no exception to this rule. Homeschooling is simply more convenient for a family on the road.

This is especially true if you are the kind of family that does not spend a large chunk of time in any one place. Being on the go is not that conducive to the time commitments that schools will expect. The good news is that homeschooling is not some lower quality of schooling you have to settle for because of your lifestyle. With the right mindset and parental commitment, homeschooling can be a great choice among the many available educational options.

In Chapter Three, we discussed how many families have joined the education revolution through one form of homeschooling or another. While unschooling falls under the wider homeschooling category, we will address it more specifically in Chapter Seven. This chapter will specifically discuss the more structured forms of homeschooling in relation to travel. For world schooling families, it is the combination of world travel with education that makes homeschooling truly revolutionary.

Structured Adventurers, then, are families who use a more direct, methodical approach to education while traveling long term. While they are all about the adventure of seeing the world and living outside the box, they still see the value of providing some sense of formality and – you guessed it – structure to their child's education.

Many parents will combine more structured homeschooling methods with a touch of unschooling. Many see the younger years as a time to teach the basic skills of reading, writing and arithmetic, requiring a more structured approach to at least those topics. Other parents have certain skills in mind that they would like their child to master. For instance, the Prince family (whose story we learned about in the last chapter) determined that language was a priority for their family and planned accordingly. Here is how Ariel Gibson, a world schooling mother, explained her approach:

> I decided at some point that there are things I really think are important for my daughter to learn, and we do formal lessons on those things. I always try to make it fun (games, workbooks she likes, songs, hands-on learning), and then I let her do her own thing the rest of the time. We do everything together because she's an only child, and I often find that she learns a ton just through everyday conversations and experiences with us. But it did not sit right with me not to teach the things I felt important.

> She's an avid reader, and I insist that she read some about the culture we are visiting. This really does enhance her experience there. We do it together mostly. We learn science and history about the area so we know what plants we can eat and what the people before us did. I help her learn the tools of writing because she wants to be a writer. I help her with math because this is important and useful in everyday life. I insist she play an instrument because I see the rewards of her creativity and skill with that. I see her joy when she accomplishes a beautiful song, and I push her when practicing is hard.

> I waffled on these things for so many years because I didn't settle on one philosophy, and I found that we both felt better with a little bit of formal lessons and then lots of life experience. It helps us to have a routine somewhat, and she really gets so many ideas and jumping off points from the things we do together. When she says she needs more free time, we slow down. I see her feeling accomplished.

> This could happen for a child who is self-motivated, or one who sets goals and works towards them. And maybe we never fully unschooled so it didn't take hold in my kid. Either way, I feel good about what we are doing and the lifestyle we are giving her. I think every parent has to sort out what works for

their family and their conscience. I'm happy for the people who unschool and love it. This is just what we do. I also have seen that if I provide enough resources, my kid gets interested in a thing. For instance, I bought a workbook on constellations and before I could say anything my daughter took it and did the whole thing. Now she's schooling me. My daughter is 10.[43]

I feel this is the perfect balance for the Structured Adventurer. Structure is great, but if taken too far it can actually interfere with what a child can learn from their experiences traveling the world. Thus, this type of world schooling parent has both the structure and the adventure. For some, however, it does take more of a conscious effort to not go overboard with the structure. Nancy Sathre-Vogel had this advice for the Structured Adventurers among world schooling families:

> I'm just going to be really upfront here. My personal feeling is that when people are out traveling, especially long-term [and are only] using a pre-printed curriculum... It goes contrary to basically everything we are doing. The message we are giving our kids is, "I know that we are right here, two miles from the Panama Canal, but before we can go and see the Panama Canal, which is all fun and games and it's interesting and exciting, we have to do the real school. And the real school is when we open our workbook and it says we are on page fifty-six today and so we have to be learning about the American Civil War. And so, here you are, two miles from the Panama Canal and you're learning about the American Civil War. That makes no sense.

> I just say this because there are a lot of people who really don't trust themselves and want that pre-printed workbook that lays everything out for them, rather than trusting their own gut – rather than being willing to say "You know what, learning about the Panama Canal IS school and qualifies as valid learning...

> Now, a lot of people do get creative. They feel like they need the curriculum, so they actually look for curriculum about Egypt and they're reading books about Egypt when they are in Egypt and they're doing activities about Egypt when they are in

Egypt. [So while] they do look for pre-printed curriculum, they use it as it ties in to the country that they are in.

Still, there are a lot of people who want to go traveling, but they can't give up that idea of formal curriculum. [Unfortunately,] the message that they are giving their kids is that where they are isn't valid, [it] is not school, it's not education, it's fun and games and the real school is sitting here at this table doing this workbook before we go there. And that just doesn't make sense and it's not the goal we're going for. We really need to empower [ourselves] with the idea that we don't have to be constrained to a curriculum. Our travels can be our curriculum and that's okay. That works just fine.[20]

It all comes back to balance. Set curriculum can be very beneficial for learning, but we should not cling to it as if it is the only real way learning can actually happen. As we discussed in Section One, it is important to realize that the system in which we were educated is flawed. The system's dependence on curriculum is largely arbitrary and geared toward test preparation. That is not the kind of education your child needs. And, as a world schooling family, you are in a position to give your children a level of education so far beyond workbooks and textbooks.

So, what are the best strategies Structured Adventurers can use to find that perfect balance between structured learning and adventure? There are actually quite a few exceptional strategies in this particular camp, which is what makes this whole world schooling adventure so exciting! Here are just a few:

Parents As the "Teacher"

I have to put "teacher" in quotation marks here because the parent's role is often more as a facilitator or co-learner than as an actual teacher. This is especially true if you are the kind of parent who is sensitive to your child's interests. Still, Structured Adventurers do maintain a certain element of parent-directed learning, at least when it comes to insisting that your children learn specific skills and subjects.

As we learned from Ariel, there may be topics that you feel strongly that your child should learn and you will likely take a more direct approach in teaching those skills. This will not always include a workbook or textbooks, but it can. Here is how the Oxenreider family from The Art of Simple approached homeschooling while they were on the road:

> When we are in one place for more than a week at a time (our preference), we'll spread out and open our backpacks a bit to dig in to our books. Our priorities are our field trips and adventures, obviously, but this sort of learning fits in to our nooks and crannies:

> Our oldest, turning 10 in a few weeks, journals our outings and adventures, doubling as both writing practice and creating the perfect souvenir for our trip. She also writes down Bible verses from our family devotional time, jots down new-to-her spelling words from books she reads, and publishes occasional blog posts.

> Our middle, age 7, practices his handwriting with his workbook and with his spelling lists, and also works on his articulation—this is one of the few "schooly" things we're intentionally doing as daily as possible because he has a fine motor and speech delay.

> Both kids are also working their way (albeit slowly) through their math that we have on the iPad, and they also keep track of their allowance on a spreadsheet with the different currencies and their value converted to U.S. dollars.

> Our youngest, age 4.5, mostly plays, but since he loves "doing" school with his older siblings, he'll practice his letters when the workbooks are pulled out.

> His brother and sister also enjoy helping him with counting and sorting (coins! rocks! steps on the Great Wall! whatever we find!).

> We also listen to Story of the World as a family from our iPad (doing our best to listen to the ones pertinent to where we are), and we reference our travel map near-daily and talk about our

locale's language, politics, food, animal and plant life, geography and culture.

The older two read a ton on their Kindles, which are gloriously connected to our local public library back home.

We continue our family read-alouds via Kindle as well, and take advantage of any picture books that might be near us (we've stayed in guest houses with libraries, and a few rental houses have had kiddo books).

And just like in real life, the kids play, play, play.[44]

Besides ensuring that your children are learning certain subjects, parents can also encourage their children to learn about the places they are visiting in relation to various subjects. You can have your children keep a travel journal to practice their writing, learn about the ecosystems in the surrounding region, study the architecture of the world's great buildings, observe the art, history, religion and geography of whatever location you may be at, and on and on.

While Structured Adventurers follow the homeschooling method of more parental input into what a child studies, the world schooling spin on homeschooling may end up looking nothing like traditional homeschooling. And while children may be learning the same subjects taught in a traditional school setting, their understanding of those subjects will go above and beyond anything that could be taught in the classroom. Not only will children be learning each subject in relation to all the others but they will also be learning them *in context*.

External Teachers

Now, not all parents are ready or capable of teaching their child everything they feel they need to know. And even when a child is largely self-directed, some parents may not have the time, knowledge, patience or resources to teach every possible subject. Though our children may not believe it, we parents do not know everything.

And while we always have Google and our own burning curiosity about life and learning, it is also important to remember the tried and true economic principle of specialization. If we all focus on what we do best, we can build on other's strengths to obtain the best from everyone. When it comes to world schooling, this means being willing to consider tutors, local teachers, and collaborating with other parents within the world schooling community.

Collaboration can come in many different forms, from offering classes within world schooling groups on social media, to traveling with a group of world schoolers and hiring a tutor to work with the children on a group level. Local teachers can be found to teach everything from weaving to metalwork, and from robotics to marine biology. And online tutors are available to teach just about anything these days. Just take a look at the experience of Brandon Pearce's daughter:

> My oldest is taking private voice and songwriting lessons through Skype with a professional songwriter who lives in LA. She's been doing that for a little over a year, maybe two years now, and is loving songwriting. She is so passionate about it. She even has three songs that she's professionally recorded and they're up for sale on iTunes and Spotify. And she's writing a lot more at the same time. She's got such a gift for it.
>
> We first noticed her talent for it when we were in Barcelona where we were renting a place for a month and she just surprised us with this song she wrote. We said, "Really? You wrote that? That's really good!" And she wanted to do more with that so we found her a teacher after that. She also plays guitar and she's taking violin lessons as well while we're in Victoria. She really wanted to study violin and choir, so now she's in a local community choir.[4]

The thing I find so exciting about this story is that the ability to pursue this passion for music with such dedication is something that Brandon's daughter may not have had in a regular school situation. She may have been able to pursue her musical interests at after school programs or through school choirs, but such programs would not be as personalized to her needs and interests.

Furthermore, she would either have to limit the amount of time she could dedicate to such pursuits to compensate for the typical school workload, or allow her life to be consumed with extra curricular activities. With the freedom of homeschooling (and world schooling in particular), Brandon's daughter can pursue what she is passionate about at a much deeper level.

Hopefully, this gives you a taste of the possibilities that are out there. In reality, there are so many ways to capitalize on other's strengths to boost your child's educational experience that there is a whole chapter in this book (Chapter Eight) in which we will discuss the many different educational resources available to world schoolers, including those for finding the right tutors and local teachers.

The truth is that every Structured Adventurer has to find the right approach for their family. Rather than telling you the right way to be a Structured Adventurer, let's end this chapter with a couple stories from families who have chosen to combine education and adventure in their own unique way. I am sure their stories will inspire you as they did me!

Jennifer Miller

Question: How did you begin traveling and world schooling?

Answer: My story is a little different from the other families [who world school]... I was raised pretty non-traditionally as well. My parents took me out of school two separate years and we traveled. So, from the time I was young, travel was a part of my life. I don't ever remember a time that included less than three countries or three languages in my sphere. To an extent, I was world schooled as a kid. Although I also attended traditional schools because homeschooling wasn't legal in Canada when I was a child.

[I got] my degree in education and, long before I had children, I remember the day I came home from school and told my husband that if we had kids, "I don't know what we're going to do, but it's not going to be this." We didn't have kids yet, but I knew that I wasn't going to subject them to that kind of education.

But knowing what you don't want to do and knowing what you do want are two very different things. So, that started me upon a seven-year journey of reading and researching and trying to understand what the different philosophies were. I had a great education in boxed education, from having had one myself as a child in public schools to a degree in education. I understood what everyone thought that education should be. But when that's not what you want, you have to re-educate yourself.

Our kids have never been to school and we never intended them to go to school. We just began with them as babies and have worked our way through. They are now 14, 16, 18 and 20, so the oldest two are finished, the younger two are still in process.

We homeschooled them. Our philosophy in general was a blend of the classical and Charlotte Mason methods. My goal in educating my kids was to raise the bar. We're homeschooling our kids because we believed we could do better than public school; we wanted more for them. We wanted a broader, more liberal education. I'm a firm believer that the classics are part of that, but they're not the sum total of that. It's a pretty terrible, dry, boxed way to learn if that's all you do is a classical education. So we blended that with travel.

When we took off traveling in 2008 we were going to ride our bicycles from London, England to Africa and back... And we did that. We rode our bikes from London to Africa and back. That was also the year the economy crashed in the United States – well, worldwide – and we lost all the money we had saved. We'd spent a lot of time saving and working so that we would have the money set aside to do that year and when we were in Italy it all disappeared. So, we had to decide at that point if we were going to go back and get jobs and carry on with life, or whether we were going to, in some way, reinvent ourselves.

What we ended up doing was going to Africa and living as inexpensively as we could for winter and just working really hard at reinventing our careers and that has allowed us to continue. We have been traveling pretty much full time since then. About a year ago we sort of settled on Wolf Island, but our friends laugh when we say settled. We spend about half of our time here now. My guys are, right now, on a sailboat heading to the Bahamas for the winter. And I have been here exactly two weeks. So, settled is relative. Basically, we've been traveling full time ever since and blending our kids' education with the travel we've been doing. It's been a good way to spend some time with them.

Question: Would you have started traveling when your kids were younger?

Answer: I'm Canadian and my husband is American, so we traveled [quite a bit] just because of … our family structure. Our kids had been to Mexico and Hawaii and all over the United States and Canada since they were babies. So, in that sense we did travel, but we don't call that our travel because we still had a home base. But by most people's standards we've always traveled. We talk about our travels beginning in 2008, but really that was after lots of other stuff. We did a 500 mile bike ride through the Maritime Provinces of Canada, my husband and I motorcycle road tripped to lots of places. It's just on a sliding scale of what travel means.

Question: If you had to explain your educational methods in as few words as possible, how would you describe or define them?

Answer: At the most basic level, in terms of the choices that we've made for our kids, I'd say that it is parent-directed, child-centered learning. I'm not an un-schooler. I don't believe that kids just inherently know everything that they need to learn and should just be allowed to follow their passions without any kind of outside structure. I'm a big believer in insisting on math and science and grammar and those kinds of things, but it can be done in a way that is delightful to the child.

When they were little, the thing that we were concerned with was just building their basic skills. And that involved everything from learning to care for their own bodies and the houses we were living in to basic building blocks of language and science and math. And so we did a lot of work in those areas, both formally and informally. As they have gotten older, they get a direct say in what they learn.

For instance, my two sons who are working through their high school equivalent of work, they know every year that they have to choose a math, a science, a language, and a history or culture subject. We've got our structured things in the sense that you have to choose one of these things, but within that there's a lot of latitude. They can study a lot of different things. This year they're both doing a course on seamanship and small boat handling because, obviously, they're sailing to the Bahamas and back, so that's practical.

They're doing a course on climate change because one of the things that has been a take-home message from our travels abroad is the way in which the world is changing and I think that's going to be one of *the* defining issues of their generation. It seems to me something that's important that they learn and they're interested in it. And then they continue every year with formal writing lessons because I just don't think that you could ever possibly become a perfect enough communicator. We could all stand to do better.

Question: Have your methods changed over time?

Answer: Oh sure! Because children change over time... One of the big shortcomings of public education is that it is tempting to standardize everything. You've got to work with the kids that you've got every year. You've got to work with the parents you've got on a given year and the family situation. Obviously, the way we schooled when we had a house in New Hampshire with a purpose built school room is very different from the way we schooled when we were road tripping across Borneo and living out of our backpacks for two years in Southeast Asia. It's really important to adapt your methods to the real world, whatever that means for you.[24]

Daniel Prince

Question: How did you begin traveling and world schooling?

Answer: We were living in Singapore. We'd left the UK in 1999 and so we were living in Singapore for 15 years. The thing that took us there was my career at the time. We left the UK when we were 22 years old and with the remit to do a two year contract in Singapore. That turned into four years, which turned into six years, which turned into marriage, which turned into 4 kids, which turned into 15 years and culminated in something needing to change.

The country had changed, the business that I was in had changed, everybody was getting moved around. It was strange times from the knock-on effects of '08. It had become untenable for us to stay living there because all the prices were skyrocketing there. Everything had changed.

From a personal point of view, as well, having four kids and being at work all day long at the office, you're not seeing them, you're not spending time with them; they're growing up under your own nose. You're kind of a weekend lodger and then you're gone again. I wasn't really enjoying that role, so we decided, "Let's get going."

It was after I read the book "The Four Hour Workweek." That was the catalyst, it made me look at life differently and try and challenge myself to find another way. And we did. After two or three months, we came to the realization that this was something that we wanted, it was something that was achievable, and what was to stop us, really?

It's not like we followed the book in every detail. I didn't invent a muse or have an income revenue stream yet. I didn't start my business, it was just more the point that the message was to try and break break free from something that's not working for you anymore, rather than just sit there like everybody else who will be there for the next 20-30 years. I didn't want that. At the time, I was 38 and I could not envision myself in the same role for the next 20-30 years. That was just an awful thought. It was more just a real jog [to realize], "Change your mindset, figure something out, get going first and you'll figure something out along the way."

... The way we did it, we home swapped our way around the world.... when you get to these places, of course you want to make the most of them and discover as much as you can and get out there and immerse yourself in the culture and find the historical [and] touristy things to do and the best way to learn about the country. We were on the go completely for two and a half years and now we're at the point that we're here in France, and we're sitting still for nine months.

The kids are really happy and we've got them in a school. It's the first time they've been in a school for 2 1/2 years. They've really enjoyed that transition, they're really coming along with the language, they've loved socializing and making new friends.

Question: Were you homeschooling your children as you were traveling?

Answer: Yes, we were. We started homeschooling immediately, pretty much as soon as we took them out. We went to our home in Ko Samui in Thailand for two months. We found that by sitting down with them one-on-one (or one-on-two) for 45 minutes or half an hour or whatever you could squeeze out with them, there was far more [progress].

To give you an example, [before] they would come home from school and it would be evident that whatever they'd been taught during the lesson hadn't sunk in and they were getting frustrated and they couldn't do the math sums. And then you'd sit and help them to try and overcome it and try and get to the answer, but you would be teaching them how you were taught or how you remember it, which is completely different to how they're getting taught in the classroom. So, it's just a complete compounding mess.

Whereas, if you sit down on-on-one with someone, you can figure out, "Okay, they're still not getting the answer, so we've got to change tactics. We've got to figure out where it's breaking down. Where's the hurdle that you're falling at? And if you're falling at that specific hurdle in the sum, then we work around that. We work backwards from that, back to the start and then we'll get back across the hurdle and get to the final answer. Because everybody learns differently.

Generally, there's three or four different ways to do a sum. Everybody has a specific way of learning, but in a classroom they'll just wave this magic wand and everybody has to learn it that way, even if it doesn't resonate with you. We found a great uptick in their confidence, with everything, with spelling, with basic writing, with math in particular with our oldest one who used to fear it and hate it and now really loves it. That's been the biggest takeaway for us for homeschooling.

And then the word world schooling didn't really exist to us two and a half years ago, but that slowly started creeping in. We belong to different Facebook groups. World schoolers, they call themselves. You are literally teaching them as you're on the go. As you're in Rome, as you're in the Colosseum, you're learning all the historical stuff and the geography that goes hand in hand with that. And again, teaching that stuff in a classroom, kids are just going to switch off. But if they're there in the belly of the beast, looking at the arena, trying to imagine lions and tigers out there, you have such a better hope of getting through to them and making it all stick in their minds.

Question: If you had to explain your educational methods in as few words as possible, how would you describe or define them?

Answer: World schooling definitely covers it. I heard somebody say "edventure" – that's how it was for the past two and a half years. There would be days where we would sit down and pull out text books, but the majority of it was on the go and learning through experience.[5]

Chapter Seven: The World un-Schooler

My younger brother did not love school. In fact, sometimes he would even say that he hated it. Over the years, his boredom from sitting in a "box"' all day and his frustration with the inefficiency of the typical school model of lectures and homework were common complaints in our home.

Even though he enjoyed some of his classes, he felt he could be more productive with his time and actually learn without sitting in school, "doing nothing" (as he liked to put it). I struggled to understand the sentiment for many years, but I could tell my brother's dislike of school did not translate into a disdain for learning.

While he would put off half-heartedly finishing a math assignment until the morning it was due in class, he would gladly spend hours studying the geography of the Rocky Mountains and plotting out every mountain range in our region. He would often summon me over to the computer screen where he had pulled up Google Maps and zoomed in on a section of a certain mountain range.

He would then go into a detailed explanation of how he had calculated the slope from the image and how he knew that the incline of the mountain was suitable to a beginner versus a black diamond ski route. Once, he found an area that he was positive had the adequate snowfall and variety of different slopes and terrains perfect for a new ski resort, he would then drag my parents up into the mountains to study the area in person.

He would do the same thing with the weather, incessantly checking weather reports and studying every climate prediction he could find online, on the radio, or even through phone calls to local weather stations. He would then calculate how much snowfall was needed in a certain area in order to sustain the perfect ski conditions for the longest period possible. None of these activities had anything to do with school.

I often watched my brother and thought what a shame it was that what he was doing was not considered, by most, an "education." Not even he thought of it that way. Nothing would go on his high school transcript about his unique and specialized skills. And no test would adequately illustrate to a college admissions board how incredibly smart he was.

But that did not matter. Just one look at my brother and I knew that he was going to be successful in whatever he chose to do. He was passionate about the things *he* chose to learn and teach himself. And he really *was* learning – not in school – but naturally through what I have now come to know as the educational method of unschooling.

My brother was directing his own learning, in the context of his passions, without the aid or direction of an educational institution. Without knowing it, he was unschooling himself.

Unschooling, or Growing Without Schooling, is a homeschooling method that has been around for several decades. We looked at it briefly in Chapter Three, but barely scraped the surface. So, before we get too far ahead of ourselves and look at the incredibly powerful way unschooling fits into world schooling, let's take a deeper look at unschooling on its own.

In its simplest form, unschooling is "to live as if school does not exist."[45] Beyond this definition, it is difficult to describe unschooling precisely because it is the least formal and structured educational option available to parents and children. As Ben Hewitt points out, unschooling is difficult to describe with accuracy simply because it has no set definition. But this is a desired characteristic, he argues, because "Unschooling cannot and should not adhere to any particular definition. It should be as fluid, imprecise, and individualized as the families and children practicing it (p.17)."[6]

What *can* be described, however, are the deeper philosophies at the foundation of the unschooling movement. Unschooling is grounded in the belief that children have an innate drive to learn and that they are fully capable of self-directed learning. Peter Gray said it best when he explained:

> Children are biologically predisposed to take charge of their own education. When they are provided with the freedom and means to pursue their own interests, in safe settings, they

bloom and develop along diverse and unpredictable paths, and they acquire the skills and confidence required to meet life's challenges. In such an environment, children ask for any help they may need from adults. There is no need for forced lessons, lectures, assignments, tests, grades, segregation by age into classrooms, or any of the other trappings of our standard, compulsory system of schooling (p.6).[3]

Unschooling parents possess a simple trust in a child's instinct to learn and grow. They recognize that each child will advance at their own pace, but that they *will* advance as they discover themselves, their interests and their needs in order to function and succeed in life. It often takes a lot of faith and patience, but unschooling parents trust that their child will learn what they need to learn, when they need to learn it "even when it seems as if they are falling behind the manufactured expectations set by institutionalized schooling (p.72)."[6]

This belief is rooted in the deeper philosophy that the most important lessons any of us learn are learned from life itself. Unschoolers, more than any other group, see school as an abnormal environment in which unnecessary adult direction and confinement inhibits a child's natural curiosity to ask their own questions and explore and pursue their own interests. Life is the teacher and the world is their classroom.

But how exactly does learning take place? many ask. In her Unschooling Handbook, unschooling veteran Mary Griffith explains that her children's "'lessons' were simply side effects of the way they spent their time."[36] If life is the great teacher, then how you and your children choose to live your lives will largely determine what you will learn. This is true whether you choose to unschool or not. Unschoolers simply take a more conscious approach to this life truth and harness it to achieve greater learning.

Without a conscious effort to utilize life's profound educational power, we may be teaching our children all the wrong lessons without even knowing it. How do we choose to spend our time? Who do we choose to spend it with? What do we do to make the world a better place? How do we contribute to community? What value do we place on family and relationships? We teach our children these things and more by the way we choose to prioritize our lives, no matter how we choose to educate them.

Unschooling, then, is merely just a recognition of this truth and a more attentive approach to life so that our children's learning can be elevated to the max. When we can achieve this as parents, we open our children up to an accelerated path to learning. As Ben Hewitt explained of his boy's learning, "When they are granted the freedom to follow their passion, they learn quickly. I almost wrote "effortlessly," but that's not true. Their learning isn't effortless; it merely appears that way, because they do not struggle against it (p.141)."[6]

The answer to the question of how learning takes place for unschoolers, then, is that it happens all the time. As children are allowed the freedom to learn, they become more in tune with their own curiosities and more capable of seeking out the resources to help them answer the questions that truly interest them. Those resources can take the shape of books, adults or even classrooms if the need arises, but unschoolers are not confined to those resources alone. Unschooling is a mindset that is not limited to any one way of learning.

Amy Sztupovszky from World School Adventures, described the unschooling approach this way:

> Unschoolers are using all the means at their disposal from libraries, to community classes, to art galleries, to museums, to local mentors. Unschoolers are using their communities as their classrooms. Unschooling parents are watching and listening to their children, and when we see a spark of interest we are there to help facilitate that learning by helping with finding books, classes, YouTube videos, and mentors to help our children to pursue their interests.[46]

Emily Horos, another unschooling parent, had this great advice to give as well about what unschooling is and is not:

> One thing to remember is that unschooling doesn't mean "no rules." Set limits on electronic devices. Require socialization. Assign chores that require skill development. Last month our 6-year-old got to plan a weekend trip. He had to stay within a budget. He spent days going online and researching, reading reviews, doing math for the budget, using a map to plan the route... it was great. He learned a lot and felt like he was getting to do something special.[47]

While unschooling is child-led, that does not mean that the parent does not play an important role. You are there to support and facilitate, and sometimes even set limits. Those are all crucial responsibilities to fulfill and ones that often take up more time and effort than expected. Ben Hewitt clarifies:

> There's often a misperception that unschooling parents don't do much. That they just let their kids run willy-nilly while the adults go about their days. That unschooling is, when all is said and done, easy. In this family, at least, nothing could be farther from the truth. In this family, unschooling is not easy, or convenient. It demands significant reservoirs of thought and patience and... presence (p.102).[6]

Your role is critical. It may be different from the typical teacher-student relationship, but it is just as important, if not more. If you are new to the approach, it may take some time to adjust to your new role. Among unschoolers, this process is known as deschooling and includes the time it takes to study and really understand what it means to unschool, accept the philosophy and decompress from the mentality of the traditional school system. For many, this process takes approximately a year for both parents and children.

Unschooling will often look nothing like school and that can be hard to adapt to, especially if you have grown accustomed to the traditional school system. Yet, learning is happening. You just have to take the time to see it.

When Unschooling Meets World Schooling

How does unschooling fit into world schooling? And what is the difference between the two? To begin, just as unschoolers are part of the larger homeschooling community, parents who choose to unschool as they travel the world do so as part of a larger world schooling community. We have already seen that there are many ways to worldschool our children – from being Settled Globetrotters to Unconventional Traditionalists to Structured Adventurers – and World un-Schoolers form a vital part of this larger community.

Of all the world schooling methods that we have discussed so far, World un-Schoolers embrace the most atypical approach to schooling. Unschooling, in and of itself, is a total break from the traditional school system. Adding travel into the mix means World un-Schoolers are a truly singular group of parents and children blazing a completely new educational path into the future.

Just as travel adds a priceless element to all the other approaches, unschooling becomes truly powerful when it is combined with world travel. A common strategy used in unschooling to pique children's interests is a term coined by Sandra Dodd called "strewing." The idea is to strew interesting things along our children's paths that they can then choose to pursue or pass by depending on whether or not it interests them. Lainie Liberti explained this concept to me in an interview and then expanded on the idea to show just how powerful unschooling can become through travel:

> As an unschooling parent, you would look at your six-year-old little girl and see that she is dancing around, loving the dance, dressing up like a ballerina and making costumes out of whatever. Instead of telling her what to do next, you leave little pamphlets of the ballet performing the Nutcracker on the dining room table or a flyer from a dance class.
>
> You never say to your child, "Oh, since you like dancing, would you like to take a class? You just don't do that... You leave these little clues so that they can discover and make the decision themselves. Because, even though you believe as a parent that you know them the best and that you have their best interests at heart, if you make a suggestion, you are almost imposing what you think they should be learning.
>
> The whole idea of unschooling in that manner is to allow the child the control and the power and the decision-making and to have that experience doing so. The strewing process is tricky and you have to be really delicate with that, but with my son and I, we've noticed that the world strews *for* us as we're traveling...
>
> We are allowing the world to strew.
>
> I never knew before we started traveling that I had an interest in archeology, but the world strewed that and it just happened.

That's why I think that world schooling is so powerful. You're exposed to so many things.[29]

And that is really where the magic lies. When you choose to travel, the world not only becomes your classroom, it becomes your teacher. The places, the history, the people, the languages and the demands of a traveling life, all contribute to a learning lifestyle beyond anything your child would ever receive within the four walls of a classroom.

But what exactly does a World un-Schooling lifestyle look like? As I mentioned earlier, no two unschooling families will look the same or take the same path. That is the beauty of it all. However, I have found it helpful to read about how other World un-Schoolers go about their day-to-day activities just to get an idea of the many different possibilities. For that reason, the rest of this chapter contains the stories and experiences of three separate families who have adopted the World un-Schooling lifestyle.

Nancy Sathre-Vogel

Question: If you had to explain your educational methods in as few words as possible, how would you describe or define it?

Answer: What we did was just use what was around us. Let me give an example of that with the Panama Canal. If we're arriving at the Panama Canal, that is, in and of itself, this huge thing that you can dive into. You can learn about the history of the Panama Canal, you can learn about the economic aspects of it. That canal cut a *week* off of the journey. Boats used to have to go all the way around South America and now, all of a sudden, it was a week shorter. What are the economic aspects of that? By cutting a whole week off, that boat can now make two trips in the time it used to take to make one trip. [The economic implications are] huge!

[You can also study] the ecological aspects of connecting the two oceans. Looking at the physics of raising those ships up and lowering them down. Looking at the gates themselves. Just those gates! Do you realize how much water those gates are holding back? Those gates are phenomenal. They are absolutely incredible. So, looking at the physics and the science involved in those gates is just remarkable.

There are so many different aspects of the Panama Canal that you can look at. My big thing is "use what's around you as the basis for the education. Don't be afraid to throw out the curriculum. Don't sit there and study the Civil War because your child happens to be on page 56 of their textbook. If you're at the Panama Canal, then learn about the Panama Canal!

Question: Did your methods change over time?

Answer: Yes, they did change throughout our trip. At the beginning (again, I had just come out of teaching) I was more geared toward me as the teacher and them as the students. As time passed, I realized that we were simply a team working together and learning together and I really didn't even worry about it. I was curious!

One of the examples that I often give is that all the way from Mexico down we had been seeing these little shrines on the road wherever anybody had been killed in a car accident. When we got to Argentina, we started to see bright red shrines with flags. I saw these and thought *What is with all these red shrines?* So, when we got into town I researched it and there is this whole huge story with an Argentinian folk legend. It's a fun story that is really neat.

So, again, that curiosity... I'm the one who sparked that. I don't even think that my husband or boys had even recognized that there even were these red shrines. They hadn't even made that connection and I wanted to know *What is this?* So, as a family, [we] went ahead and took this journey into this Argentinian folk legend. And it was wonderful. But it was because I was curious. Toward the end it wasn't like I was leading anything, it was based on anyone asking a question and that's where we went.[12]

Question: Have you been traveling ever since your first trip to Panama?

Answer: A lot of things have changed since then. First of all, we started homeschooling and trying to replicate the school system at home and follow a system, but we quickly learned that that was not working for us. Our kids just weren't getting into it. We weren't really into it and we weren't as close as when we were doing the six weeks in Panama.

It was around that time that we discovered the unschooling movement – the idea of child-led learning and allowing our kids to learn what they're interested in and facilitating those passions with resources and encouragement. So that's kind of the direction we've taken since then, but the first few months in Costa Rica is where that all started.

Question: What does unschooling look like for your family?

Answer: Right now, it's quite eclectic. All three of our kids go to a democratic school once a week, every Tuesday. I don't know how to describe it, but it's kind of unschooled based in a way. The kids do what they're passionate about. For example, if the kids want to cook something they'll all walk to the store and buy the ingredients and then come back and cook it together. That type of thing.

They recently had elections. There are only twelve students in the school, but they had elections because they are interested in that process that's going on right now. So just different things like that. And there are teachers there to facilitate a lot of the learning opportunities that they have, but there's a lot of discussion and communication and voting and different things to help make sure everyone's needs are heard and met.

The girls wanted that even more for the socializing aspect than for the educational aspect because we have been traveling quite fast-paced for a long time. We've plunked down here in

Victoria, Canada for six months this year to settle in a bit more and develop some friendships and give my wife and me a chance to work on some of the projects that we want to do a little bit more. So, that's one of the things that they're doing.

They were also taking ice skating … and my middle daughter is in gymnastics. She's really into that. We don't have a very good floor for it right now, but when we were in New Zealand she would spend hours a day practicing on her own and watching YouTube tutorials.

YouTube is a place our kids go for a lot of their education. They just search videos on how to do this and how to do that and they figure out things. They also use sites like Khan Academy and there are several apps like Epic App for Reading. My middle daughter just finished a series of 20 books.

Philosophy-wise, it's more about not really telling them what they need to learn, but trusting that they'll learn what they need to learn and supporting them in that. And, of course, we do provide some encouragement and some suggestions here and there, but we don't like to force education on them.

Question: So, when they do have an interest in something, how do you help facilitate?

Answer: With ice skating, they said, "We're going to Victoria, let's learn to ice skate!" They know it's colder in Canada and it's a western country and they have ice skating – and they really miss that being in the tropics so much – so we found them a class (and it was very affordable here, actually) and we signed them up for it.

With violin, my daughter came to me and said, "Dad, I really want to learn violin and we've been traveling so much and it's been hard to find a teacher, but I know that we're here for six months and I really want to do this. She actually looked up online and found a teacher for herself and one of us contacted the teacher. So, she found her own teacher and that was kind of cool.

101

Sometimes, we'll see an opportunity coming up and I'll let the kids know about it and ask if they're interested and they'll say yes or no.

Question: Do the locations drive the topics, or do the topics drive where you decide to live?

Answer: It depends and it changes. When we started traveling it was more about the locations and going to places that really excited and interested us. And I guess that it still is to a degree, but after seven years and 32 countries, it's less about going to a new and exciting place and more about going to visit people that we know there or joining a community that we're interested in joining.

That is one of the reasons we came back to Victoria because we knew that they had such an active homeschooling community here and we wanted to take part in that. The same with Bali, there's a great community in Bali as well and our kids have made friends there. In fact, our middle daughter's best friend lives there, but she's from Sweden and we'll be going to Costa Rica this April and meeting her there. And then we're going to be staying with them in Sweden next summer. So, a lot of our travels revolve around people and community.

When we're going to a place for short term – a month or two – typically we do like to look and see what classes and opportunities are there educationally, but depending on our energy levels and what we just came from. For example, we're here in Victoria now for six months, really full-on with classes and a whole lot of stuff right now. The next place we go, I'm thinking we're probably not going to do very much. We're just going to enjoy being there. We might go out and see a few things, but I don't think we'll necessarily get involved in weekly classes or that type of thing unless there's something that's really exciting for them. But I'm thinking that we'll be happy to have a little bit of a break from that.

Question: Are there specific things that you have tried to teach your children even though you are using the unschooling

102

method? For example, are there certain things that you say "I want to make sure that you learn 'this'"?

Answer: In a way. It's funny, though, because the same things I want to teach them are often the things they want to learn. I asked my kids the other day what they feel is lacking in their education — "What do you feel that you need in order to be able to survive in society?" — and my youngest who's only five didn't have much to answer, but my oldest two said, *We want to understand taxes. How do you pay taxes and how does that work?*

So, we'll be looking up some videos — I already found one for them, but we haven't watched it yet. But things like that financially... I do think that it's important to know financial math and that you understand how to earn a living and how all that works. You could say that I try to encourage them, but they are also bringing it up.

There are times where they'll ask me a question (especially when they were younger), *How many days until my birthday Dad?* And rather than just answering the question I'd say, *Well, let's see... What's today? When's your birthday?* And I'd try to help them figure it out themselves. I would encourage them to solve their own problems rather than answering the problems for them.

Question: What is one word or phrase you would use to describe what you do?

Answer: Interest-led learning.

Question: Do you feel like your methods will change going forward or do you feel like you've come to a place where you've found what works for you?

Answer: I have no doubt that they will change again. I do not want to live in a fixed box of *This is the way we do things in the world and how we'll always do things.* They will definitely change and we'll stay flexible as our needs shift. I guess that's one of the other things I've learned from travel is that whenever I make plans, they usually end up changing. I can't plan, I can't predict as well as I'd like about what I think the future will hold. Life goes more smoothly when I don't resist and I'm more flexible.[4]

Lainie Liberti

Question: How did you approach education when you first started?

When my son and I decided together about eight months into our travels that there was really no reason for us to go back, ... at that point I had to then do the responsible thing and look at education as something that I was accountable for. I had to make sure he was "educated." So, I assumed, *Okay, we're going to keep traveling, we're going to do it, but now I have to 'educate' him.* And that's when I started researching all the different methods and everything I could about alternative education.

That's when I discovered that there was a thing called unschooling. And the more I read and the more I became involved in the online community groups – reading blog posts and listening to podcasts and reading everything that I could get my hands on and then asking questions – the more I realized that we were already doing it. We were learning naturally.

I also realized that this whole concept of self-directed learning was a brilliant concept and I didn't have to learn how to do it. And not only was my son learning so much from the world (and I had seen him grow leaps and bounds in just the eight months), but I had also noticed and reflected that I was doing it too. At that point, we decided that we were going to be partners in learning. We were already partners in travel, we were partners in budget, we were partners in everything we were doing anyway, so we said, *Let's be partners in learning.*

And that way, it also created this non-hierarchical approach that we took into learning. What I discovered about unschooling is that most people start with the education first and then pull those concepts into other parts of their lives, but we were radical livers before we became radical unschoolers.

We identify with being a radical unschooler by all definitions, but really we self identify as being world schoolers or radical unschoolers who travel, and we call that our brand of world schooling.

Question: How exactly do you unschool? Do you pursue certain experiences to teach you certain things or do you just let whatever happens become the lesson?

Answer: Let me make a distinction: As an unschooler, we don't divide the day into subjects and we don't create a lesson plan. What we do as world schoolers and travelers is we're very intentional about being present in our own lives and maintaining a level of curiosity about everything around us.

The curiosity is something that, because of the partnership that my son and I have created in learning, I've been allowed to tap back into my curiosity that most of us as adults tend to phase out. And I was allowed to be present and tap back into my natural curiosity. Not only did I spend time (and do spend time) daily encouraging Miro's curiosity, he does the same for me. That's the partnership in learning that the family can decide on. And it's intentional.

Can you imagine how different it is [to be intentional]? For me and my son it took traveling to get us to do this, but anyone can do this if they decide to do it in their normal life. Can you imagine how different life would be if you were intentionally present with everything that you do? And then that helps ignite your curiosity.

Question: Did you find that traveling gave you more time to be more intentional?

Answer: Oh, absolutely! Are you kidding? I gave up, I say a 9-to-5 life, but it was really a 7am-to-10pm life. My son would say to me, *You're always working, you never spend any time with me.* I ran a branding agency, I had employees, of course I never spent any time with him other than him being in the office with us. So, yes, it gave me a lot of time. It's the trade off. It's that question of what do you value? And I clearly valued my son, but it took me ten years to realize that. I really lost out on the first ten years of being present with him, but I couldn't do it anymore. I didn't want to do that life anymore.

Question: If you had to explain your educational methods in as few words as possible, how would you describe it?

Answer: Intentionally present, in partnership, inspired through curiosity.

Question: How does World un-Schooling play out during your travels? After you've gotten the curiosity about something, how do you go about learning it?

Answer: Both my son and I are experiential learners. We're people who like to do in order to learn. I can give you a million different examples of things that we've done. It's that child-like curiosity and asking. I always believe that if you just ask, the worst that can happen is a "no" for an answer.

Here are some examples: We've become passionate about archeology. We visit the sites and then research and then discover that there are alternative researchers that have theories on the sites that we've just visited that are different from the conventional history. [Once] we've discovered that through our research and we want to give some relevance to the experience that we are having, to take it even deeper we'll send them an email and ask them if they are here or wherever they are. And if they're in the same place that we are, can me meet? Can we talk to you? Can we assist you? Can we volunteer? And guess what! We keep getting "yes" for an answer!

We've been on archeological digs, we've held these crazy elongated skulls in Peru, we've walked through ancient cemeteries where we had to jump over fences with these researchers just to help them record some of this information. We've done some crazy things simply because we asked if we could. And these have been really hands-on educational experiences.

Another example would be my son's passion for learning about chemical energy with plants. We've gone out and learned that there was an ethnobotanist in the area, so we asked if we could walk through the hills with them and tag along just to shadow them. It's different than reading about it in a book. To have conversations, in context, of the things that you're interested in, that's meaningful. What's more meaningful is researching and finding out mentors that are in your area and asking the question: *Can I come with you? Can I help you? Can I catalogue your plants for you? Can I learn about your studies?*

Another example is going to a farm in Wales and learning how to build a house. My son thought it would be a really cool thing to do after watching a video. But [watching a video is] not the same thing as spending three weeks building the thing. And we've done that because that's what he wanted to do. We have so many stories. You have no idea!

Question: Does travel direct your learning or does learning direct your travel?

Answer: Both. Early on – one of the things that really opened up the world for us – we decided as a team that we were going to say yes to everything. That meant that, we were going to be directed by our interests and our passions, and also by the location where we were at because we're on a really strict budget. The bus can only take us to the next place, but if somebody asks us to veer to the right or to the left or to join them for dinner, then we're going to say yes.

Obviously, we're taking into consideration safety issues and all of that stuff, but that means we're flexible to go with the flow and to allow life to unfold in such a way that we're trusting the unfolding. There's a beauty in that and, again, that's also part of being present. Life is going to unfold.

[As the world strews for us] we're now both these wide-eyed, curious learners who are present and intentional. Some things appeal to us, some things appeal to me and some things appeal to him and some things don't appeal to me. But our agreement to be supportive and partners with each other in our learning allows us to step into the role of the supporter or learner whenever it's necessary. That is partnership in learning.

And, especially as a family, it provides an opportunity to talk about [different topics]. Every learner and every family is going to be different, but the world strewing as it will, we'll see different things. Our family probably will talk about politics and human rights, where another family might see the exact same situation and talk about architecture and fashion. And we're looking at the exact same thing.

It just depends on not only tapping into the personality of the family [but also] the partnership of the learning that you've agreed to practice together. And then, allow the world to strew in a way that's valid and interesting to you as a family or you as a learner and then either be the learner, the supporter, or both.

Question: Have your methods changed over time? Or have you kept the same approach over the years?

Answer: The partnership is lovely and nothing has changed in terms of that. What has changed are the interests and the content, but we're pretty practiced at being present and being curious and being supportive. One of the things that we practice is non-judgement. Learning, as in life, is all about practice. You're never done with learning. You're never done with living until you're done, of course. But learning especially, you're going to be a learner for the rest of your life if you're lucky.[29]

Section Three:
Making it Happen

Chapter Eight: The World at Your Fingertips

FLOOD WARNING! A flood of information is expected in this chapter. Advance with caution.

I really mean that. This chapter can be dangerous. We have made it through all the reasons why world schooling is a positive educational choice for our children and families; we have discussed the many different ways each individual family can choose to world school; and now we are about to tackle all the millions of resources available to make it all happen. If you are not careful, you can drown in all of the information.

This chapter is meant to be a springboard for discovering the many educational resources that we have, literally, at our fingertips. I add the warning because it is all too easy to get lost in all of the educational programs and shiny objects that are out there. If you do not have a strong vision of what you want to achieve through world schooling, the overwhelming supply of resources can take over the more important goal of learning. Jennifer Miller had some wise words to share on this topic:

> People get it backwards: they focus on resources instead of philosophy and then they try a bunch of stuff that they end up frustrated with because it's not a good fit. To me, it's a much smarter approach to carefully define what your philosophy is [and] what you are trying to accomplish, because when you begin to look at various resources it becomes obvious that it's going to be a good fit or not.

For instance, somebody that is an unschooler is probably not going to go for a science course that requires them to buy a microscope and a dissection kit and to work through the book in a certain way. I mean, maybe they will. Maybe they've got a kid who's into that. But somebody who's into classical education is going to want something that is more structured – A, B, C, D, E – in terms of building a writing structured style versus somebody that's not.

So, to me, defining your philosophy of education is the first and most important step. And then any number of resources can be found. There's no shortage online of things you can do.[24]

There really is *no* shortage. A simple Google search will bring up pages and pages of educational resources from websites to apps to books to who-knows-what. However, because there is so much out there, it is good to start with a curated list to weed out the unnecessary and go directly to the good stuff.

We will start with the educational resources for children and then we can get to all the resources you will need as a parent to keep you going and teach you more about world schooling and everything else that comes with it.

Educational Resources for Children

THE WORLD

If I have not established this point yet, then let me clarify one more time: the whole point of *world* schooling is to use the *world* as your most potent educational resource. Plain and simple.

Learn about the Roman Empire in Rome. Learn about the Vietnam War in Vietnam. Learn about ancient American civilizations in Teotihuacan, Chichen Itza, Tikal, Machu Pichu and beyond. Discover the affects of deforestation while traveling the Amazon. Be mesmerized by space with a trip to NASA. Develop a love for the arts by seeing the originals up close and personal. Learn a language by being immersed in it.

Teach math by having your children help with currency conversions and budgeting trips. Promote healthy physical activity by hiking, snorkeling, swimming, skiing, or even playing soccer with local children in the street. Replace those old "home economics" classes by learning to make tortillas in rural Guatemalan villages or sushi in Japan.

Go to where your interests call you.[48] If your children are passionate about XYZ, plan a trip to go where X is done on a regular basis, Y is in its natural habitat and Z is produced. But also let the world inspire new interests. As Lainie Liberti shared from her experience, the constant exposure to new things through travel may instill in both you and your children new questions, passions and interests. Allow yourself to be open to the journey.

The opportunities are truly endless. I could not possibly record them all here so I am not even going to try. Just let your imagination run wild. Go. Be curious. Be present. Be learners. Let the world and all the amazing people in it teach you and your children through experience and connection. It is a beautiful thing to behold!

As we move forward with other resources, just remember that everything else in this chapter may be able to supplement and enhance the learning that occurs while out in the world, but it should never be a replacement for what our children can learn directly from life and their exposure to this amazing planet.

ONLINE RESOURCES

I remember sitting in my school library with my fellow first graders many years ago and listening to a man give a presentation about technology. He told us that new, revolutionary technology that changed the way the world worked almost always shortened the time to the next great invention by approximately half.

He stretched his arms out as wide as they could go and then explained that something like the invention of the wheel would be at the far end of historical innovation and that right in the middle would be the invention of the printing press. The time to the next big invention then came only a few hundred years later. And then the next advancement came only a hundred years after that, then fifty, twenty-five, etc. Each invention made the next great technological breakthrough arrive faster and better than the one before.

"You kids," he said, "are living during an exciting era when the time in between revolutionary technological change will begin to happen every five years, then every couple years, then every year, then every few months to weekly and maybe even faster!" He finished his presentation with his fingers squeezed together showing how quickly things would be changing on a day-to-day basis.

I heard that presentation at a time when personal computers were just becoming a household item. And, perhaps because it seemed so relevant, that little library chat stuck with me over the years as I watched the world around me completely transform in the face of daily technological advancements. Computers, internet, laptops, smart phones, tablets, social media, etc. The world we live in today is almost unrecognizable compared to the one I was born into. And I'm not even that old!

What's even more exciting is how technological advancements have changed, and *can* change, education. While the change is slow in coming on the public front (as we discussed in Chapter Three), technology is increasingly empowering parents across the world to give their children educational opportunities that were unthinkable under any educational circumstances just decades ago.

Really, who would have imagined that kids — kids! — would be able to take *free* computer programming or animation classes from the comfort of their own homes? And these are not just your typical run-of-the-mill animation classes (if any animation class could really be considered "run-of-the-mill"), these are classes offered by Pixar![49]

And that is not even the tip of the iceberg! That is just a tiny little snowflake sitting on top of the digital revolution occurring within the world of education. It is so exciting! But here is the thing, technology has to be used the right way. If not, it can be just as destructive as the iceberg that took down the Titanic. Salman Khan, the founder of Khan Academy himself, even warns against the improper use of technology in education:

> Let me stress ENLIGHTENED use. Clearly, I believe that technology-enhanced teaching and learning is our best chance for an affordable and equitable educational future. But the key question is how the technology is used. It's not enough to put a bunch of computers and smartboards into classrooms. The idea is to integrate the technology into how we teach and learn; without meaningful and imaginative integration, technology in the classroom could turn out to be just one more very expensive gimmick.

Duke University professor Cathy N. Davidson has written that "if you change the technology but not the method of learning, then you are throwing good money after bad practice…. [The iPad] is not a classroom learning tool unless you restructure the classroom…. The metrics, the methods, the goals and the assessments all need to change (p.122)….

It was never my vision that watching computer videos and working out problems should comprise a kid's entire education. Quite the contrary. My hope was to make education more efficient, to help kids master basic concepts in fewer hours so that more time would be left for other kinds of learning. Learning by doing. Learning by having productive, mind-expanding fun (p.149).[10]

While Khan's arguments speak to the classroom model of teaching, there is so much we can take from his perspective on the place of technology in education. It is not the solution in and of itself. It is a tool that can be used poorly or leveraged to help children master the learning process. With that advice in mind, let's take a look at some of the best online resources for world travelers looking to get a top notch education on the road. In lieu of the most recent quote, let's start with Khan Academy.

Khan Academy

Hands down, Khan Academy is the most recommended online resource I have seen in the world schooling community. Does that mean it is the perfect resource for everyone? No. But it is easy to see that Salman Khan has an incredible vision for online learning. While researching this book, I was able to interview one of the software engineers at Khan Academy who gave me an inside look into the goals and opportunities provided by Khan Academy.

While it began with math, the site already has a large coding platform, the previously mentioned
Pixar in Box program, a "LeBron Asks" segment with LeBron James and exploratory physics, and topics anywhere from economics to science to history to English and more. The five to ten year goal is to have a complete K-12 curriculum.

The site has received wide approval from generous donors all over the world, which is one of the big reasons the site is already available in several languages besides English, including Spanish and a project to translate all content to Hindi.

You can access Khan Academy on a regular computer, or there are phone and tablet apps that increasingly include the same content and capabilities as the online platform. If you're going to be traveling without Wifi, you can download videos before you go to ensure continual access on your journey.

The exciting thing with Khan Academy is their commitment to providing free access to quality educational material while pushing the limits of how education even looks and takes place. They have a team of people who are actively researching how kids learn math and how they can better tap into intuitive things as they are learning. While a lot of it is exploratory, it is a great indication that Khan Academy cares about doing things right.

[Side note: I have no affiliation with Khan Academy (or any of the resources mentioned in this chapter) and have not received any monetary benefit from writing about them, I just really love and believe in what the organization is doing.]

But you do not have to take my word for it. Daniel Prince says that Khan Academy is his family's absolute favorite learning resource. He explains:

> The time and effort [Salman Khan] puts into these videos… and he puts them out there completely free! He's possibly the best math teacher that anybody could ever ask for and he's just out there doing it for free. It taught me so much about math because I was learning at the same rate as my daughter was when we were sitting down together doing these math problems.

> We would go to Kahn Academy together and watch a video on it. Then I would say, *Okay, long division. I get that now.* And then, if she didn't [understand], we could just go back and rewind and watch the video again and find the part that she wasn't understanding. [We could] pause the video and talk about it between us and see if we couldn't figure out a way to get her to understand it. And, yeah, no problem. Long multiplication,

same thing; order of operations and more. So, without a doubt, my number one tool is Kahn Academy.[5]

Starfall

Starfall is a publicly supported charity that creates free and low-cost opportunities for children to successfully learn through exploration. Their free website, starfall.com, provides meaningful and fun learning opportunities, while a $35 home membership reinforces Starfall curricula so children can learn anytime and anywhere. Membership includes teach.starfall.com where lesson plans and other educational resources may be found.

Curriki

Curriki, a non-profit, hosts a free library of 83,000+ educator-vetted learning materials in all K-12 subject areas and in many formats–including individual lesson plans, instructional videos, units, games, and simulations. Content contributed by educators and select partners is available to others for use, adapt and share at no cost.

iTunes U

While the program can be used in K-12 classrooms and colleges to track homework and grading, iTunes U can be a great tool for the Structured Adventurer who wants to have a more hands-on way of following their child's progress through certain subjects. You can import your own material to share with your children or take advantage of the free course from the best colleges all available through the program.

Open University Courseware

Universities have begun to create open courseware programs that are available to anyone and everyone. MIT Open Courseware publishes material from 2,340 of its courses online. For the self-directed individual, this can save tens of thousands of dollars and potentially many years. Taylor Pearson tells the story of a young entrepreneur who did just that:

Scott Young... put himself through the entire MIT course material in twelve months for two thousand dollars. He bought the textbooks and was able to get all the classes online. This education at MIT would have cost around $150,000 and four years of his life. Instead, he was able to put himself through the entire course material in twelve months for $2,000. That's around 98.7% cheaper than the cost of a degree from MIT, not including the three years he saved.

In a world without the internet, where information was expensive and the only way to learn was to get a degree, that made sense. In a world with the internet, where information is rapidly approaching free, it's hard to rationalize spending money paying for access to general knowledge when you can get the same knowledge for free (p.132).[17]

Many other top universities offer similar open online courses, such as Stanford and Harvard. Other programs can be found on sites such as The Great Courses, Coursera, edX and Academic Earth.

Secular Homeschool

SecularHomeschool.com is the web's largest social community and information resource for secular homeschoolers with over 30,000 registered members from all over the globe. Families frequent SecularHomeschool.com to search the directory for secular homeschooling curriculum, to find secular homeschool support groups in their area, and to network with other like-minded homeschoolers. All the articles, directories, and forums are accessible on both desktop or mobile, meaning you can find the information you need wherever in the world you happen to be!

K12 International Academy

K12 International Academy is a fully accredited, US diploma granting, private online school offering full-time and part-time study. They offer an American curriculum online for students under the age of 21 worldwide, where not restricted by local or country-specific policy/laws. The K12 curriculum is rooted in decades of cognitive research, while the Online School interface harnesses the power of 21st-century technology to make lessons and learning come alive. They provide their students with teacher support and all necessary materials required for the school year.

TED

You may already be familiar with TED Talks and local TEDx events. These videos are a great resource for both parents and children to learn about some of the most fascinating topics out there. The organization has also begun a new initiative entitled TED-Ed, which brings together educators, students, animators and others to create a powerful education community.

Google Scholar

Google Scholar is a great jumping off point for all your higher level investigations. This can be a great source for parents who want to know the facts about education, child development, etc., or the perfect resource for older students learning to write their own research papers or simply learn more about a given topic. While Google Scholar does not provide instant access to every scholarly article out there, it provides a wide selection and can lead you to the journals that you may eventually want to purchase to further enable a child's passion through research.

Teaching Textbooks

Teaching Textbooks features an audio/visual math-learning style unlike any other. The interactive lectures, engaging lessons, and step-by-step solutions allow independent learners to teach themselves while on the go. With an easy-to-navigate website, along with online and offline versions, Teaching Textbooks makes a great travel companion for any student!

RightStart Mathematics by Activities for Learning, Inc.

This hands-on program uses visualization of quantities and provides visual strategies for learning the facts. The primary learning tool is the AL Abacus, a special double-sided abacus. Practice is provided with math card games, which minimize review worksheets and eliminates stressful flash cards. Understanding and problem solving are emphasized throughout the curriculum. The website has information and resources for the world schooler, from articles to webinars to blogs.

Other Online Resources:

Writing/Grammar/Spelling
- No Red Ink - English grammar and writing
- Institute for Excellence in Writing - Writing
- Brave Writer - Writing
- Spelling City - Spelling
- Grammaropolis - Grammar
- Squeebles - Spelling App
- Grammarly - Grammar Website and App

Reading
- Explode the Code - Literacy
- Endless Reader - App
- LeVar Burton Kids Skybrary - App

Full Online Learning Programs
- NROC (National Repository of Online Courses) - Middle school, high school and college
- MobyMax - K-8
- Always Ice Cream and Clever Dragons
- Brain Pop - A learning resource supporting core and supplemental subjects.
- IXL - K-12
- Perfection Learning Textbooks and supplemental programs for K-12 and higher education preparation and learning.
- EL Education – Open educational resources available to parents and formal educators.
- Education.com – Pre-K–5, including free and paid worksheet downloads.

Math

- Endless Numbers - App
- Prodigy Math Game - App
- Squeebles - Math Apps

Science

- Home Science Tools - Everything science website
- Radio Lab - Podcast

Programming

- GitHub – Free programming books
- Code Academy – Free programming courses
- Udemy – Paid programming and other courses
- Team Treehouse – Paid programming and web design courses
- Code School – Paid programming courses

LANGUAGE

Personally, I loathed my language classes in school. I loved pretty much every other class I ever took over the years, but language classes caused me more grief than I ever thought possible. It wasn't that I didn't like the idea of speaking another language, it was that I could see how unproductive it was to learn another language inside a classroom.

As I mentioned earlier, I learned more Spanish in the two weeks I spent in Guatemala than my previous two years in high school Spanish classes. Then, after two more years of Spanish in college, I moved to Chile for a year and a half where I was finally able to master the Spanish language.

I simply took a notebook with me wherever I went and when I could not say a certain word or communicate what I wanted to, I would write it down in my notebook. Then, every morning I would give myself an hour to study the language and I would go over the things that I had struggled with the day before and then head out the door to try out my new skills and learn some more. What I had not been able to do in four plus years in the classroom was achieved in less than four months of being immersed in the language.

Skip those dreary language courses at home and go travel! As you do so, consider some of these online language sites and applications as supplementary resources for all of your immersive learning:

- Rosetta Stone
- Open Culture
- Duolingo
- My Daily Phrase
- Mango Languages
- Memrise

BOOKS

Books are at the heart of learning. No matter how the world changes, there will always be a place for books. Physical or digital, books should be an essential component of any world schooler's educational arsenal. For one, books are the greatest tools to teach children to read. Mary Griffith explains:

> Whatever other tools you may introduce, the first requirement is one exemplified by this five-step reading program that occasionally appears on homeschooling lists on the Internet: Read to them. Read to them. Read to them. Read to them. Read to them. It's one of the basic tenets of the whole language approach to literacy: children will not learn to appreciate reading if they never see it being used. Reading aloud will do more to turn your kids into readers than any other single thing you can do.[36]

There are so many other useful purposes for books and I could not possibly list them all here. And chances are, if you are reading this book, you already know how amazing books are and the myriad ways children can use them. So, I will spare you the lecture. Instead, let's focus on how you can ensure that you have lots and lots of books while you are out, roaming the globe.

One option is, of course, to haul them around with you. While I would consider always having a few physical books on hand, carrying pounds and pounds of books is not a very appealing option. If you want physical books but do not want the hassle of carrying them around everywhere, Better World Books is a great site where you can both purchase and donate physical books.

Another opportunity that many people do not know about is simply checking out e-books from your local library. If you have a membership to your local library, check to see if they offer e-book rentals. I did this by looking up my hometown library (even though I am thousands of miles away) and typing in "ebook rental" next to the name of the library. And, sure enough, a page popped up giving me the library access code and explaining that all I needed was my library card number to get access to all of the ebooks and audio books available in the library. Pretty neat.

There are also some really great online resources that you can use to get free or cheap access to digital books. ManyBooks.net provides an extensive library of books in digital format for free. Many of the eBooks are from the Project Gutenberg archives, which means you will be able to find a lot of classics on the site, perfect for reading on the move. Archive is a non-profit library of millions of free books, movies, software, music, websites and more.

Kindle Unlimited is another great way to have constant access to books. There are also the occasional Facebook groups that will offer you a free book in exchange for a review on Amazon or for sharing on social media. And then there are the many sites like Book Bub that pool the numerous limited-time free or discounted book deals that you can find on sites like Amazon, Nook, Kobo, iBooks and more.

For good ideas on country-specific books, take a loot at Shannon O'Donnel's list of travel books at alittleadrift.com or get the book "Give Your Child the World: Raising Globally Minded Kids One Book at a Time" by Jamie C. Martin.

PHYSICAL MATERIALS

Besides carrying some actual physical books, what else will you need to pack to ensure that all on-the-road learning is optimized? The biggest items to pack into your bags are journals. Journals can be used to write about the day-to-day activities and improve writing skills, but they can serve many other purposes as well.

For instance, children can keep a journal about nature, food, culture, fashion, languages, science, art, stories from people they meet, plants and basically anything that interests them. And journals do not have to be kept in a notebook. If they want to, you can help your kids start their own blog or keep a video journal that they could upload to YouTube, even just to keep relatives at home updated about your travels.

Other good items to pack include Kindles, tablets, laptops, a white board and markers, workbooks (for those who use them), maps, books and a few fun games. In reality, there is no need to overpack. Lainie Liberti had this to say on the topic:

> Leave behind the heavy toys and bulky art supplies. Toys can be made out of any surrounding materials with a healthy dose of imagination. Art supplies can be bought locally in almost every country, used and then left behind.
>
> The best tool for the traveling worldschooler is a dedicated laptop computer per person. This device has multiple purposes; a reading tablet, entertainment unit, drawing pad, game device, research library and communication tool all in one. I can already hear the objections from parents around the world, "I have to limit my child's screen time or they will be on their computer all day!" I would remind parents that technology is not something to be limited for the sake of limiting technology as no parent in their right mind would put a limit on "paper-time" (books). Instead reframe the conversation in your own mind to look at technology as a tool that allows us to do many things, including traveling with less.[50]

TUTORS & SPECIAL CLASSES

World schooling your children does not mean that you have to be your child's sole educator. In fact, none of us should be. No matter how smart we are, we all have limitations. When our child's interests surpass our own knowledge or abilities to help them learn a certain topic, it is encouraging to know that there are many qualified mentors our there to teach them when our personal set of skills and knowledge do not suffice.

This is a common practice among parents in the homeschooling and world schooling communities. Ben Hewitt explains how he and his wife sought out friends and professionals who could mentor their sons in subjects in which he and his wife had no expertise. He explains, "They needed someone to validate their interests and instincts, someone whose words carried the authority of experience and respect. Because let's face it: children don't always consider their parents to be [founts] of wisdom (p.140-141)."[6]

Mentors can come in all shapes and forms. They could be working or retired professionals who want to share their knowledge, or individuals you meet along your journeys who may have never finished their primary education. Everyone has something they can teach. Hannah Miller, a world school graduate, had this to say about her various teachers throughout her years traveling with her family:

> All my teachers have been fantastic. My parents are the first to come to mind, of course. But there've been so many others! Guatemalan boys to teach me soccer tricks, countless hippies to trade songs and star signs with, cooking lessons by locals, loom weaving, courtesy of a Mayan woman we befriended, and endless others! You don't have to be a certified teacher to have an incredible wealth of knowledge to share.[51]

I echo Hannah's sentiment. I received the greatest lessons about illegal immigration sitting in the kitchens of rural Mexican families as the mothers made tortillas and told stories about the family and friends they knew who had tried to enter the United States without the proper documentation. I returned to college the following semester ready to turn all those stories into full-blown research projects. More than one professor was blown away by what I had learned and could bring to the immigration policy debate from simple conversations with villagers around a comal and metate. Some of those women had never gone to school, others had made it through their primary education, and yet I consider them some of my greatest mentors.

If you are interested in learning from locals, there are many ways to connect. One online platform available to anyone is Backstreet Academy. Backstreet Academy is a peer-to-peer impact travel platform for unique travel experiences. Travelers can connect directly with a local who does amazing activities that showcases tradition, culture and craft. Impoverished communities can make two to three times their original income, be respected as masters and conserve their intangible cultural heritage.

Another great way to find mentors is through a simple Google search or through the local community wherever you may be located. Brandon Pearce explained how he and his family find mentors through this strategy:

> The world school and local homeschool groups in the places we're in are such fantastic resources. There are a lot of things that come up there that we'd never know about otherwise. In fact… our kids, the oldest two, are taking a Japanese history and culture class. And also a tech and tinker class. It's once a week and that is actually at a house that's right below us and the person on the bottom floor is the one who's holding it so they just walk downstairs to class once a week. And that's not listed or advertised really anywhere. It is online, but it's hard to find. We found it because of the homeschool group we are in and because of where we are renting.
>
> Our middle daughter was taking digital art lessons from a teacher in Germany at one point. In some of the places we go we have teachers come to the house to teach. In Bali that's fairly common. We also had a Spanish teacher in Costa Rica and an Indonesian teacher in Bali, so some of the language stuff we've gone that way.[4]

If you are traveling to a new place every few weeks or months and want a mentor on a longer-term basis, digital tutors are a great way to go. A good place to find Skype tutors is Buddy School, and other platforms like Navanas are developing and growing with the world school movement as well. You could even use freelance websites to contract experts in various fields. Get creative, keep your eyes open and you will find the right mentors.

EXPERIENCES & COMMUNITY

One of the most common concerns with any type of homeschooling – including world schooling – is the challenge of socialization. We have already debunked the myth that homeschooling somehow automatically makes children socially awkward. Even so, without effort, world schooling can lead to isolation from a community larger than your immediate family. Instead of simply sending your children off to school each day and living your day-to-day lives within an established community, world schoolers have the responsibility to *create* community.

There are many reasons why community and experiences outside of the family are so important for children. Besides the obvious reasons of establishing friendships and avoiding loneliness on the road, learning alongside others enhances learning. Not only can children learn from others' perspectives, but children can also build off of each other's strengths to solve problems and discover new things.

There have been numerous studies regarding how children learn and the benefits of children learning together. One of the greatest benefits is that they begin to teach each other, which helps both the learner and the teacher master new concepts. (For a truly inspiring story, listen to Sugata Mitra's TED Talk on the Hole in the Wall project in India.) What is most interesting about these studies, however, is that they have found that children learn best when they are in mixed-age groups – not the same-age groups you find in formal school settings.

While I couldn't possibly cover all of the research that has gone into this learning method in this chapter, I encourage you to investigate it for yourself. Mixed-age learning allows children to observe those who are more advanced than they are and to to teach those who are still learning what they already know. World schoolers can look to create these learning environments wherever they go, building communities of unconventional learners all over the planet.

One of the current leaders in this movement to create learning communities is Project World School, an organization that designs immersive learning experiences around the world for teens and young adults ages 13-25. Each retreat is between two and four weeks and provides participants with an opportunity to live and function together as a community while having an immersive experience specific to the given location.

For instance, a past retreat held on the coast in Ecuador focused on marine biology. The participants never opened a marine biology book. Instead, they were on the coast, went to the conservations, partnered with the volunteers that were working towards conservation and even worked with the Pacific Oil Foundation. They also teamed up with a local school that was helping to educate some of the kids about the ocean and even interacted with the fisherman that were there. They were not only applying all the different aspects of marine biology, they were also applying them from different perspectives.

Then, each participant also brought with them their own perspectives that they were able to share within the group as they discussed everything that they were seeing, learning and experiencing. The retreats allow participants to have external cultural experiences very unique to a specific area, which they can then process together as a community and look at all the different aspects. As a community, participants get to share and support and bounce ideas off of each other, reflect and have fun.

That is one of the biggest elements of learning that schools do not naturally tap into: having fun. This all comes together within an environment built to work specifically for the self-directed teen to create community and have an incredible world schooling experience where they can feel safe, develop a team and be able to assert some leadership, support others and have a reflective experience. They are powerful and incredible experiences.

So far, the majority of the participants come from homeschooling and unschooling communities in the United States. There have been a couple of participants from Poland and South Africa and one from Brazil. The organization is looking to have a greater international presence. Retreats have been (or will be) held in Ecuador, Thailand, the Amazon jungle, Peru, Wales, Mexico, Bali (Indonesia), South Africa, Greece and Bolivia. And the list of countries will only continue to grow.

One final recommendation of an experience that children can seek out and benefit from are internships. Whether it is freelancing, guided programs to help kids start their own blog or an apprenticeship, there is so much that children can learn "on the job" that will serve them greatly.

CREDENTIALING

For those looking to go on to college or who have the need to build a resume, credentialing is an important aspect of the educational process. If anything, many states and countries will require that world schooling parents document their child's educational progress. There are many different ways to do this and you should make sure you know what your specific state/country's guidelines are. Here are a few resources you can use to get started:

Home School Legal Defense Association (or HSLDA)

The HSLDA provides numerous different resources for homeschoolers, including educational and legal help to new and veteran homeschoolers. You can check out the home school laws in your state and find tests and transcripts. They can also write a letter that you can carry with you as you travel that states that you are homeschooling legally, which can come in handy when traveling to less homeschool-friendly countries.[52]

Homeschool Transcripts

Homeschool Transcripts is a website that provides training workshops and software that will help you plan your child's high school curriculum, document learning, prepare for college and career, present professional credentials and learn how to obtain high school transcripts.

Community College

If you want to find unconventional ways to get your world schooled children into college, I would suggest reading the book "The New Global Student" by Maya Frost. One of her big recommendations is for your child to enroll in a community college (at home or abroad). With credits from a community college, a high-school-aged student can then qualify as a transfer student when they are ready to be admitted to the university of their choice.

CLEP- College Level Examination Program

CLEP has been around for over 40 years and is accepted by 2,900 colleges and universities. The program allows students to earn college credit by getting qualifying scores on 33 different exams testing introductory college-level materials. While CLEP is widely accepted, you should check with the university where your child wishes to enroll to ensure that CLEP exams will earn them college credit at the given institution.

Peggy Webb founded West River Academy in 1993 when she couldn't find a service that would help her navigate the legal aspects of homeschooling and unschooling her daughters. She and her daughters now help parents and students throughout the world design programs unique to the interests, abilities and goals of the child. The school is fully accredited and offers its participants high school diplomas and transcripts through its Graduation Program.

Resources for Adults

Being a world schooling parent demands a lot of work, research and constant learning. The following are a few places you can look to begin your world schooling journey, find community and support, and get more ideas for your coming adventures.

BOOKS

- "Free to Learn" - Peter Gray
- "The New Global Student" - Maya Frost
- "Home Grown" - Ben Hewitt
- "Give Your Child the World" - Jamie C. Martin
- "Roadschooling: The Ultimate Guide to Education Through Travel - Nancy Sathre-Vogel
- "The One World Schoolhouse" – Salman Khan
- "The Four Hour Workweek" - Tim Ferris
- "The End of Jobs" – Taylor Pearson
- "The Unschooling Handbook" - Mary Griffith
- "Living Deliberately: Your Guide to a Ridiculously Awesome Life" – Rachel and Greg Denning
- "Homeschooling Our Children, Unschooling Ourselves" - Alison MacKee
- "The Teenage Liberation Handbook" - Grace Llewelyn
- "So You're Thinking About Homeschooling" - Lisa Whelchel
- "Homeschool Your Child for Free: More Than 1,400 Smart, Effective, and Practical Resources" - Gold and Zielinski

- "How Children Learn" - John Holt
- "How Children Fail" - John Holt
- "Books to Build On: A Grade-by-Grade Resource Guide for Parents and Teachers" - E.D. Hirsch
- "Unschooling to University" by Judy Arnell

BLOGS

- A Little Adrift
- A King's Life
- Bohemian Travelers
- Edventure Girl
- Edventure Project
- Escape Artistes
- Home Along the Way
- John Holt GWS
- Kid World Citizen
- Live Family Travel
- Living Outside the Box
- Natural Child
- Our Travel Lifestyle
- Pearce On Earth
- Penelope Trunk
- Princes Off the Grid
- Raising Miro
- Simple Homeschool
- The Art of Simple
- The Nomadic Family
- The Pioneer Woman
- The World is our School
- Travellers Point
- Vagabond Family
- Wandrly Magazine
- With 2 Kids in Tow
- World School Academy
- World School Adventures

- World School Family
- ZZZ World Ninjas

PODCASTS

- Epic Education
- For the Love of Learning – Voices of the Alternative Education Movement
- Homeschooling Global Summit
- Nomad Together
- Nomadtopia
- Ownstream

CONFERENCES & COMMUNITY

Being out on the road can often get lonely, which is why creating community is so important. Every so often, world schooling families will come together to share their experiences, learn from those who have been world schooling for a long time and participate in activities for both children and adults. The Family Summit is on its second year and the Family Adventure Summit will enjoy its first year of hopefully many in the fall of 2017.

There are many other ways worldschoolers have found to create community. Below, you will find a list of great digital communities where you can get help from fellow worldschoolers on most any issue, from where to go when at location XYZ to how to help your child who is not engaging in the experience to how to make airplanes and bumpy bus rides doable with little children.

Other families have found success in creating actual physical communities of worldschoolers – often refered to as World School Hubs – in one location. This can range from meeting up with another family or group of families for a short period of time to living in an established community of world schoolers in a place like Costa Rica or Andalucia, Spain where other homeschooling and unschooling families have congregated.

Finally, for those who want to participate in the local communities wherever they go, slow travel can be an easier way to achieve this. For instance, even though I have spent the past several years mainly in Mexico, my husband and I have moved several times.

Each time we discover new experiences and are embraced by a new community, both in our neighborhood and church. For me, being able to participate in the local community as a fellow neighbor, rather than a perpetual traveler makes the experience of living abroad more meaningful and educational.

You will find the right approach for you, your family and your needs. It may seem like a challenge to create community as worldschoolers, but it is not impossible and can be a rewarding experience.

GROUPS & FORUMS

As mentioned above, groups and forums can be a huge help for worldschoolers. Facebook groups are a fantastic way to connect to the world schooling community. You can also find great homeschooling and unschooling groups that are unique to a specific geographic area, or ones that address a more general audience and offer educational materials for a specific educational philosophy or approach.

The largest Facebook group to date is the group Worldschoolers, which you can find simply by typing the name of the group into the search bar on Facebook. I have found the group to be a wealth of information, from resources to travel destinations to finances to how to apply certain world schooling methods and more.

Other groups to consider include:

- Worldschoolers - FB
- Homeschool Creations - FB
- Simple Homeschool - FB
- Almost Fearless Monthly Travel Book Club - Goodreads
- Project World School - FB
- World Schooler Connect – FB
- Roadschooling Families - FB
- Families on the Move - FB
- World Schooler Exchange - Website
- Location Independent Families - FB

Chapter Nine: Financing the Dream

Almost every time I begin to explain world schooling to someone new, their typical response is something along the lines of, "Oh, that sounds like such a great way to educate your children, but that's a lifestyle only a few people can afford." I have to fight back the urge to yell, "Wrong!"

Is it a lifestyle that only a few people *choose*? Yes. Is it for everybody? No. But is it a lifestyle that is perfectly within the grasp of anyone who wants it? Yes!

There are a lot of misconceptions about what it means to live abroad. One of the biggest is that it is only for the wealthy, the corporate transfers, the diplomats or the "lucky ones" (p.260).[27] Not only is this a *huge* misconception, it is a limiting belief that keeps so many people from ever even considering the amazing opportunities that are freely available to them.

If you are already a world schooling family, you have probably heard the comment, "You're so lucky!" hundreds of times. What these well-meaning folks do not understand is that you are not lucky. You made a choice. That's it. That's the difference. It is not luck, it is choice.

This is especially true now, more than ever before. The possibilities to work remotely or run an online business are everywhere, giving anyone with the courage to venture beyond their borders the power to do it. More than any previous generation, we have the ability to choose how we live, work and even educate our children.[17]

That is why the first key to financing the dream to travel and world school your children is to shift your mindset to realize that this lifestyle is a choice. Then, and perhaps even more importantly, realize that not only is it possible to finance a world schooling lifestyle, but that *you* are fully capable of turning that possibility into a reality.

Once you change your view of world schooling from luck to choice and possibility to reality, there are two simple steps you can take to make the world schooling travel lifestyle work:

1) Save Money
2) Earn Money

I know that sounds super basic, but there is definitely more to it. Volumes and volumes of books (and blogs and news articles and pamphlets and textbooks and who knows what else) have been written on these topics. I will try to cover their most travel-relevant parts in just one chapter.

1. Save Money

One of the last nights I spent in the villages of Guatemala, I sat quietly and observed the families coming and going, the children playing happily and the beautiful sunset dancing off the mountainous jungle that surrounded us. I had come to Guatemala thinking I would be able to offer something to these people, but what I found was that I didn't have anything that I *wanted* to give them.

Don't get me wrong, I did feel that we were bringing something beneficial by helping them build a schoolhouse and fund their projects for clean water, better stoves that would reduce lung diseases, and improved medical services. However, as I compared the consumeristic culture of my "developed, first-world" home country to the happy faces and peaceful lives of the people around me, I almost felt afraid that our efforts to help them "develop" would destroy the simple beauty I saw in front of me.

They had family. They had God. And they were happy. Everything else seemed secondary or unnecessary in comparison.

I walked away from that experience with a newfound understanding of just how little we need in life. All we really need are the basics of food, shelter, security, clothing, transportation, education and health. And there is much that is unneeded even within those categories. Our shelters do not have to be extravagant mansions, our food does not need to include dessert after every meal, and our transportation does not have to be the latest model.

If we were all to take a step back, we would likely realize that we spend too much and do not need the majority of the things we have cluttering up our homes and our lives.

Once you realize this, it is easy to save more money by the mere act of spending less, buying less, owning less, and even getting rid of your stuff with a garage sell or through online markets. Simplify. And if you do not know where to start, there are hundreds of books and blogs out there that will teach you how to do it. As my mother always says, "Dare to dump!" Be honest and ask yourself what you *really* need. You will be surprised by how much unnecessary stuff you have and how much better your life is without it.

For the things that you do need, there are a million and one ways to save money on the essential purchases as well. Unabashedly make use of all the coupons out there with sites and apps from Groupon to coupons.com to the Krazy Koupon Lady and more. Take advantage of sales and special offers, but *only* if you actually need the item on sale. If you don't need it, don't buy it. Don't buy it!

Other world schooling families have great advice in this regard. Amy Sztupovszky shared some of the ways she and her family have learned to save money so they can afford to travel three to four months every year:

> My advice to those who want to travel AND have a home is to get out of your mortgage as quickly as possible. Sell the big house, downsize, buy a fixer-upper, move to a cheaper part of town, or a cheaper part of the country! If that is not possible then buy a home that you can rent out as a vacation rental while you are away or find some other way to have someone else pay at least part, if not all, of your mortgage....
>
> One of the biggest ways we can save money for travel is by living small. We reject consumerist culture and prefer to shop at thrift stores and garage sales. We grow a lot of our own food, raise chickens for eggs, and have raised pigs and chickens for meat. We do our best to spend less so we can save more and spend our money on what makes us truly happy.[53]

This is yet another mindset shift that many of us still need to make. What makes us truly happy? And are we making a conscious effort to dedicate our time, money and resources to achieve whatever that is? It all comes back to choice. Are we making the decisions that will lead us to the life we want? It may seem like a sacrifice to save, but if it enables you to live the life that makes you happy, then it is worth it.

The best news of all, however, is that traveling can also help you save more of your money – or at least make it stretch much further. You can save at home to prepare for your travels, but despite the belief that travel is expensive, you can actually live on much less while traveling the globe with your family in tow. The catch? It does take a little bit of work and know-how.

The basic and not-so-difficult part of saving money while living overseas is that living costs can be dramatically lower. Living in Mexico, I pay the same amount for a nice apartment as I did for a run down room in a shared apartment in college. Every once in a while, I will look at the cost of rent in my home state just to get the satisfaction of knowing that I am paying roughly 25% of what I would be paying in the US for a similar place.

While it was tough to pay for such accommodations when I was working for a local company that paid me a local wage, the moment I began to freelance at normal U.S. pay rates, I was able to put away more than 50% of my paycheck each month – a huge blessing, to say the least.

But it is not just lodging that costs less abroad, food is cheaper too. You can get a fantastic meal for two to three dollars anywhere from Thailand to Vietnam to Mexico or Nicaragua. I grew up with the belief that eating out was the fastest way to waste your money (and your health) because it was expensive and unhealthy and you could eat much better at home. And I still hold this belief.

However, what I have found living abroad is that this rule does not always apply in other countries. While you have to be careful with street vendors, there are so many healthy, cheap food options practically everywhere you go. And this doesn't just apply to eating out, my grocery bill for a family of three matches about what I spent on myself, alone, during college.

The list of ways you can save abroad doesn't stop there, either. The Unconventional Traditionalists reading this book will be happy to discover that they can enjoy lower costs of schooling while living abroad as well. Cliff Hsia shared how his family spent a fraction of what they would have spent on education by living abroad:

I think there's a misconception that travel is expensive with kids, or just travel in general. Traveling abroad actually can be and is very cheap if you're mindful of your budget and how you're spending. In ten months, traveling to ten countries (six of those countries in Europe and a majority of our time in China), I calculated our expenses [and] it was about $40,000 with two kids, [$3,300 of which we spent] sending them to schools for six of those months.

That came out to be about $130 a day, including all expenses, flights included. On a per day basis that is actually less than what we would spend living in the Bay Area of California – probably by half at least. So, in terms of actually financing the trip, it wasn't too bad because we were able to save up that money and budget accordingly for that.

With the schools specifically, comparing to what the costs were for every country, China was probably the cheapest. One of the schools we sent them to was a little over $100 a month for all day, five days a week, and then Barcelona was a bit more expensive, around $400–$500. In general, none of the schooling costs were more than what we would pay in the United States. And, in some cases, they were a fraction of what we would pay, almost a tenth of what we would pay. So, there are inherent savings there with putting your kids in schools abroad.[40]

On the flip side, Maya Frost explained how her family was able to save enough for one daughter's college educational expenses for every year they lived abroad. They were able to save around $3,000 a month and spent less than $2,000 a month for a lifestyle that included luxuries they never enjoyed in their home in the United States (p.15, 239, 259).[27]

She also shares the great advice that travel should be an adventure for kids. They should not expect fancy hotel rooms every night. If you travel on a budget, they will have many more adventures that they can tell stories about for the rest of their lives. Otherwise, travel will become that expensive luxury that everyone else seems to think it is and the adventure will be spoiled (p.236).[27]

How do you go about getting that cheap (or free) accommodation to save more money while you travel and inject even more adventure into your world travels? Thankfully, you have a lot of options. Lucky for us, savvy world travelers and smart business people have gone before us and developed incredible services that can help us all travel for a fraction of the cost. Many of these services are built around the sharing economy, while others are simple solutions that have been around for years.

Here are just a few of the ways that you can get free or cheap accommodation while traveling:

Housesitting/Pet Sitting

You can stay in some pretty amazing places if you're willing to take care of someone's home, and maybe even their pets, while you are there. On most housesitting websites, home owners can list their homes for free, while house sitters pay a small membership fee (as low as $20 a year). Here are some of the most well-known housesitting/pet sitting online platforms out there:

- House Carers
- Luxury Housesitting
- Mind My House
- Rover
- Trusted House Sitters

Couchsurfing

If you do not mind staying in a home while the owner is there, you can try couch surfing for free accommodation as well. Home owners will list whatever they have available – a literal couch, air mattress, bedroom, etc. – and you just select the location and "couch" that works best for you and your family. While most traveling families will probably need more than a couch to sleep on, hosting is also a great way to invite world travelers into your home (as suggested for Settled Globetrotters in Chapter Four). Here are some of the websites that you can check out:

- Couchsurfing
- Hospitality Club

Home Exchange

If you own a home, a great way to get accommodations wherever you travel is to simply swap your home with other home owners around the world. Common home exchange (or home swapping) sites include:

- Home for Exchange
- Home Exchange
- Home Link
- IHEN
- Love Home Swap
- Stay4Free

The Prince family used this particular strategy to home swap their way around the world. Daniel Prince gave us an inside look at how they did it and an extra tip on the utility of maximizing the sharing economy:

> We weren't flying from hotel to hotel to hotel; we were trying to line up home swaps with people. We had a holiday home in Thailand that we put on a home swap website, which got a lot of interest from people, and that's how we started planning our itinerary. If somebody approached us from Australia and we wanted to say yes we would say, "Let's go to Australia!" We'd start in Sydney and then try and get Perth two weeks before that and Melbourne two weeks after that and Queensland the two weeks after that. And so we'd just try and plan this whole thing. That became my day job, to find homes…
>
> When you look back at when we were first making this decision and we were doing the research… we just started scratching around the surface and all of a sudden [we found] all these families that ARE out there, living the way that we wanted to live, traveling all over the world, making it work for themselves by the sharing economy. It just seemed like endless opportunities, endless options that you had never really given any thought to.

There are so many different Facebook groups that you can join of like-minded people that you have an instant community that are more than happy to help you out. We joined one called Families on the Move and there are 250 members and they are all still traveling or have traveled and have great resources and can recommend you places to go and websites to use for your flights, recommend you houses, invite you to stay with them! It's crazy!!

… Leverage the sharing economy in any way, shape or form that you can because there is a way you can do it. I guarantee. If you need to rent a car, I bet you that there's a sharing economy carpool rental that you can use rather than Avis or Budget. If you want to swap your home, that's what we did: over 50 swaps over 15 countries and three continents and [we] saved an absolute fortune on our travel costs.[5]

Work Exchange

Another way to get "free" accommodation is to volunteer your services in exchange for a place to stay (and sometimes food). Services can include just about anything, from web design to washing dishes to farming. This can also be a great learning experience as a family, connecting you to the local communities and people – something you would never get staying at a hotel in the tourist district.

- helpStay
- HelpX
- Workaway
- Working Traveller (This site will also connect you with people who are willing to pay you in cash for your services.)
- Worldpackers
- WWOOFING (worldwide work on organic farms)

Farm Stays

Unlike WWOOFING, where you exchange your work on a farm for your lodging, for a farm stay you will actually pay money to spend the night (or week, month, etc.). Prices vary according to location, but they're usually similar to what you'd pay for a cheap hotel.

- Amish Farmstay
- Farmstay Accomodation Guide - New Zealand
- Farm Stay Australia
- Farm Stay UK
- Farm Stay US

Short-Term & Vacation Rentals

Another way to get cheaper accommodation is to use short-term rental sites such as Airbnb. These sites will usually cost you much less than a hotel, but more than what you would pay for a long-term rental.

- Airbnb
- All The Rooms - (searches several of these sites at once)
- Kid and Coe - This site is particularly family friendly and will tell you how many rooms are for kids or babies and what supplies are available, such as cribs, highchairs, etc. They also do home exchange.
- FlipKey
- Home Away
- House Trip
- One Fine Stay
- Preferred Residences
- Rental Homes
- Stays
- Sublet
- Tripping
- Vacation Roost
- VRBO (vacation rental by owner)
- Wimdu

Camping, RVs, Bikes, Boats and More

I love camping! There is a lot of adventure to be had while camping. Plus, for some reason, food always tastes better around a campfire. Camping is also a cheap way to travel. In some places, it is completely free, and when there is a fee it is usually pretty low. Just be realistic about how much camping you and your family can do. It may have been fun to camp long-term in your solo days – and it can be fun with kids along for the journey, as well – but be realistic about how much and for how long camping will be fun for the whole family if you are planning to travel long-term.

While camping sites can easily be found along your journeys, one fun camping website is CampSpace, where you are literally camping in someone's backyard. One of the big benefits of camping this way is that you will often have access to internet, which is especially nice for those who work and travel.

Many world school families also consider themselves roadschoolers, which often involves some form of traveling with an RV, bus or even bikes across continents. Those who choose to bike will still have to find accommodation, but both RVs and bikes are a great way to save on flights and other transportation.

Another way to get free accommodation (usually in exchange for work) is to work on a boat, yacht or cruise ship. This may not work for families with small children, but you never know until you try!

Discounted Airfare and Transportation

There are also lots of easy ways to get deals on discounted airfare and other forms of transportation. I'm positive I will not be able to cover them all, but hopefully this will give you some good ideas to get you started.

When it comes to buying airplane tickets, it can sometimes feel like an art or an extravagant bet. Depending on your location and the time of the year you plan on flying, it is better to buy early – usually three to six months before you plan to fly. For most flights, however, the experts say that the sweet spot is six weeks, which is when prices drop below the average fare.

On the betting side of things, it sometimes works to buy late, even just 24 hours before you plan to fly. If an airline has not filled a flight, they will often drop the price 24 hours before take-off to try and fill the final spots. I am definitely not the betting kind since the last time I tried this I ended up paying triple the regular price. However, if your schedule is flexible, you can always get on and see if you can find anything last-minute.

As with most things, it helps to shop around. Sites like Kayak help you know when to buy, based on their device that tracks the changing flight prices. Other sites like Skyscanner can help you find the cheapest days to fly (among other things), and many sites like Airfare Watchdog will send you alerts when prices drop or there is an especially good deal. Additional flight search engines to keep in your back pocket are Momondo, Cheapoair, Jetradar, ITA matrix, and Google Flight Search.

Also consider flying on discount airlines. They can really cut the cost of travel. Whether you go discount or otherwise, search for flights in incognito or private browsing mode since the cookies in your browser will recognize that you are searching for a flight and almost always make the price go up on your next search trying to get you to panic and buy before the price goes up again.

If you have the time, check the prices for your flight even after you purchase. If the price drops within a certain time frame of your purchase, you can either cancel (usually within 24 hours) and repurchase or simply request a refund. The website Yapta will actually track airfare prices for you, even after you buy your ticket, and notify you if the price drops. They will also help you claim your refund through the site.

Other secrets to getting cheaper flights include purchasing round-the-world tickets, booking separate connecting flights yourself for longer journeys with layovers, paying in other currencies (if it is cheaper), leaving on a weekday, searching for deals in the morning and being flexible with your departure and arrival dates.

It is probably common knowledge that red-eyes are the cheapest flights, but if you are traveling with kids this can actually be a big blessing because they can sleep through the flight. If your kids do not do sleep and flying, then usually the first flight in the morning will be the next cheapest option, followed by flights around lunch and dinnertime.

It also helps to search for flights for a family as if you were traveling solo. Airlines will often sell you all tickets for the highest price. So, even if one of the seats you purchase only costs $300, if the most expensive seat costs $400, you will be charged $400 for each seat.

Another tip for finding cheap flights is to search for airline error fares. Airlines will sometimes make a mistake when listing the price of a flight and you can take advantage of it. You can either search for these error fares on your own on search engines like Skyscanner, or use sites like Secret Flying that specifically post error fares their system has identified.

Last, but not least, is to use rewards programs. Frequent flier miles can be an enormous help for getting free or cheap flights to pretty much anywhere. Different credit cards will offer miles to different airlines and each has its own special perks. It is worth it to check these programs out, especially if you are a frequent traveler. You can also use the points in many of the programs for other purchases, from putting your "points" towards paying off your bills to getting special deals. Just another great way to save.

Beyond getting cheap airfare, it can also help to reduce the cost of other forms of transportation. If you are not opposed to carpooling (or if your family would fit in a car with other riders), there are plenty of RideShare websites and apps out there that you can look up depending on your location. In other areas, you can rent out someone else's car for weeks at a time on different peer-to-peer car rental sites for much less than a typical rental agency. I have even seen apps for peer-to-peer bike rentals, something my bike-loving husband has taken a great interest in to avoid the high cost and hassle of transporting a mountain bike through the airport.

If you are interested in capitalizing on the sharing economy, fellow world schoolers have begun a website entirely dedicated to helping world schoolers connect and share. World Schooler Exchange is a platform for people using the world to educate themselves and their families through travel. It allows individuals and families to swap homes, rent homes, arrange house/pet sitters, work exchanges and more.

There is also a Resources section with lists of schools, retreats and summits relevant to traveling families. Rather than just the usual house swap for a week or two, here you will find swaps for people who want to spend a bit longer and totally immerse themselves in a local community. Everything there is useful and relevant to making your global learning experience easier, helping you connect with other world schooling families around the world.

Finding Free/Cheap Activities and Entertainment

Beside the costs of accommodation and transportation, another area where a lot of people end up spending a lot of money is on activities – especially the touristy ones that other people willingly hand over wads of cash to experience. For the savvy traveler, finding great activities for a good price should not eat into your wallet.

First of all, many activities that cost an arm and a leg in places like the US or the UK are dramatically more affordable in other areas of the world. Going to the movie theater in Mexico City costs $2-3 per person for a new release. You would be hard-pressed to find a price like that for a matinee for a movie that has been out for months in the US. You will find that other activities and entertainment from ice skating to musical productions will also be much cheaper than anything you could find back home.

There are also many ways to enjoy completely free activities. Walking tours, beaches, hiking, museums (if you go at the right time), visiting religious sites, people watching and more can all be free. When you are in a new area or know you will be visiting a certain location, just look up the free activities you can do there. You will be surprised by how much you can do without paying a penny.

Travel Budgeting

My final tip for saving more money is simply to budget and track your expenses. This is an important step to saving before you ever leave, but it should never be forgotten once you are out on the road either.

Before you go, you will need to take into consideration several different factors when determining how much you will actually need for your travels. If you will be working on the road, you will have the added benefit of continual income, but you will also need to take into consideration the costs related to your work needs. Will you need WiFi? How often? Will you need constant access to a phone? Will you need to spend time at a co-working space or café to focus on the tasks at hand? All of these things will require time, money and careful planning.

You are also likely to have some expenses before you ever hit the road. Among these are travel insurance – including medical emergency and evacuation – storage fees and insurance, flights, vaccinations, visas and travel gear. You will also want to notify your bank that you will be traveling since you do not want them to freeze your account when they see purchases being made from Timbuktu. Once you are on the road, be prepared to pay bank fees for ATM usage and to deal with withdrawal limits (which usually vary on a country-by-country, or even bank-by-bank basis).

You should also notify your credit card company. Be aware that, depending on your credit card, you may be charged international purchase fees. Many cards will not charge you this fee, but it is always good to check. If your current card does charge international purchase fees, it is usually pretty easy to get an upgrade.

When planning out your expenses, keep in mind that prices can change dramatically according to location. You may be able to keep your expenses around the same by staying in nicer places in cheaper locations and then roughing it a bit in more expensive countries, but just remember to be realistic about the places you and your family are willing to stay.

And do not budget out every single penny. You will want a nice cushion of savings that you can dip into in the case of unexpected events or emergencies. In fact, as an extra precaution, have some extra savings in the bank and a stash of your home currency on hand at all times.[54]

The good news is that you will be free of many of the typical household expenses that come with living in one place. Electricity, water, car insurance/maintenance/registration, mortgage payments (if you sell or rent your home), home owners insurance, household maintenance, gas and all those other monthly bills will be gone once you hit the road.

It may take some time to adjust to a traveling budget, especially since many of your expenses will not be fixed and will vary from month to month. It may also take some time to get used to buying groceries in another country and figuring out how often your family will eat out or decide to cook a meal at home. Some of these things are difficult to know until you go simply because each family is different. Learn to track your expenses and you will get the hang of it.

You will be pleasantly surprised by how much you can save by making the decision to leave it all behind, live your dreams and go see the world.

2. Earn Money

Now, for the fun part! How do you earn the kind of money that you will need to afford a travel lifestyle? We have already debunked the myth that travel is inherently expensive, so how much you will actually need may not be the astronomical number you had in mind before you picked up this book. Nevertheless, travel does require *some* money. And, even if you are saving oodles of cash by following all the suggestions above, it is pretty difficult to save money if you have not made any in the first place.

For the most part, there are two approaches to money and travel that world schooling families take. The first is to save up beforehand and then travel full-time without working. This can take many shapes and forms in combination with any number of jobs, but the general idea is to work really hard for several months out of the year and then to take that money and travel for the other months. This is often a strategy used by Settled Globetrotters who have a home that they return to after their travels where they will repeat the process of work and travel, work and travel.

The second approach is to earn money while you go – whether that is with some form of passive income or working while you travel. The growth of the world schooling community is due, in large part, to the enabling power of the internet to help families earn money on the road. There are many ways to do so and this section is just a quick peek at some of those ways. Hopefully, it will give you just enough vision to go out there and make something happen for yourself and your family.

As we review the different options, keep in mind that most world schooling families have found that the best way to maintain their lifestyle is to have multiple streams of income. You may also find that one option is a great way to ease your way into the work/travel lifestyle, but that another option would be a great long-term project that you will want to start working towards today to sustain you in the long run. You decide.

Online Work

My life in Mexico took a giant financial leap forward when I discovered the world of freelancing. Up until then, the only way I had ever imagined I could earn money in Mexico was to work for a

Mexican employer, earning a regular Mexican wage. Thanks to that mentality, I was a college graduate earning $5/hour! Granted, the cost of living in Mexico is much lower so we were not living in poverty, but life was not necessarily easy.

When I had my son, however, I decided that I was done with working outside the home. Someone had asked me to edit a book they had written while I was on maternity leave, so I spent my hours recovering sitting in a comfy chair next to my son's crib, reading and editing the day away. While I offered that service for free, I enjoyed the work so much that I figured surely *someone* would pay me to edit for them.

I had been editing since I was little, sitting alongside my mother who often edited books for friends in her writing group (which included published authors and English professors). Over the years, I had numerous opportunities to edit essays as a college teaching assistant, and every now and then people would hand me their books and ask me to edit them – which I always did for free. But could I get paid for it?

That is when I discovered freelancing. I do not know why it took me so long – I had always dreamed of a job I could do from the comfort of my own home – but there it was! I hopped on the many freelancing sites and began to look around. And editing wasn't the only thing available; there was writing, data entry and analysis, graphic design, web development, SEO, marketing, translation, public relations, social media specialists, software engineering and on and on. I could not believe my eyes!

I was fortunate to find long-term work right off the bat editing material that dealt directly with what I had studied in college. That eventually led to writing and managing other writers, learning the ins-and-outs of WordPress and even traveling to the other side of the world. It was a dream come true.

But why do I tell you all of this? Now that I have been part of the freelance world, it seems so normal to me that I have begun to think that everyone already knows about it. But they don't! I see people asking all the time about job openings in X place and I am reminded of where I was just a couple years ago, bound to the mentality of location-based living. It doesn't have to be that way!

You have skills that people are looking for and are willing to pay you to do remotely. If you are new to this, as I was, the suggestion I always give people is to simply get on the freelancing websites, read their "How It Works" pages and start looking for jobs for which you feel qualified. And then apply! Apply! Apply! You can find projects that last one day, one week, one month, one year or beyond. Again, you decide. To get you started, here are some of the biggest freelance websites out there:

- Freelancer
- Freelance Writing Gigs
- iFreelance
- Project4Hire
- People Per Hour
- SimplyHired
- Toptal
- Upwork (previously Elance and oDesk)
- 99designs (for freelance designers)

Remote Work

If you already have a job that you love, is there a way that you could do it from home? Perhaps you have always done your job at the office, but if you were to stop and think about everything that you do, how essential is that office to your job? What would you have to change to make things work? If you are really serious about world schooling, talk to your boss to negotiate a remote work arrangement. You may feel hesitant about this, but you would be surprised by how common it is these days. Plus, your boss may be happy with all the savings that come with housing one less employee.

There is always the possibility that your boss will say no, but that does not mean you cannot work remotely. It may require changing some of your responsibilities, getting a remote work position with another company, or even switching careers and doing something completely different. You may be at that point where you are ready to start something new, but you may not and that is fine.[55]

Whatever you do, be intentional about it. If you want to travel, are you willing to make some sacrifices with work or try something new? Or do you love your job enough to stay put if that is what is required? You decide.

Online Business

We discussed in previous chapters how our children need a different kind of education to prepare them for a world that is shifting into an entrepreneur economy. While we want to prepare our children for the future, as adults, we are already living in and dealing with this shifting economy. Luckily, going into entrepreneurship for ourselves can not only be a great way to teach our children but also one of the best ways to sustain a world schooling lifestyle.

Never before has entrepreneurship been so accessible. It still requires a great deal of work, but the cost of going into business has never been lower. With access to the internet, budding entrepreneurs can easily connect with expert consultants and a growing online talent pool to help build their business, not to mention millions and millions of potential clients. Not only can you and your business be location independent, but your clients and customers as well.

Even more importantly, it is increasingly easier and more profitable to reach niche audiences that were impossible to serve without the internet. You may think that *you* could never go into business or that there is not enough demand for the services that you offer, but with the increased accessibility to the tools of entrepreneurship and the broad influence of the internet, it is possible to reach the people who are searching for exactly what you have to offer.

What is even more exciting is that, because of these structural economic changes, it is not only possible to develop and run businesses built on your passions and the principles that will benefit society, but you will also find more success and profit if you do so. Doing something you are passionate about will also make it easier to push ahead when the challenges of running your own business begin to mount. In our interview, Brandon Pearce explained the importance of going into business for your passions:

> I run up against this [problem] a lot with people who want to create businesses because they're asking the question, "What can I do to make money?" "What product can I create that people will actually buy and will want to spend money on?" But I think that is the wrong question because, being in business for that reason,

you're going to burn out. You might make money, but if your heart and passion aren't in it, it's not going to do as well as if it is.

I would encourage people first to look at your income source as — not what someone else says will help you make a lot of money — but something you feel you could put your life into and dedicate yourself to, but make it one that you can do from anywhere where you can be location independent.

There's no get rich quick option, except for the lucky few. Otherwise, it takes a lot of time and effort and consistency and putting in the work day after day, hour after hour to build the business or the product and to market the business and the product that's going to sustain you.[4]

Think about it: What are you passionate about? How can you turn that passion into a business? Can that business be run independent of location? Are you willing to do what it takes to make it happen? If so, you are already on your way to creating a source of income that can sustain your family's travels.

Ideas range from creating an app, selling a physical product on Amazon or other online sites like Shopify, selling an MLM product about which you feel passionately, writing a book or course you can sell online, coaching, consulting, teaching, starting a blog, web advertising, and many other service-based businesses.

Brick-and-Mortar Business

If you have an "offline" business, there are ways to make it location independent as well. Maya Frost's husband was able to put his wholesale product business online in just a few days. Everything was made virtual, employees worked from home and, within two months of moving abroad, his sales had doubled from the previous year (p.236).[27]

If you are looking to do the same thing, Andrew Henderson at Nomad Capitalist has some great advice on turning any business into a location independent business. The first step, again, is to change your mindset and realize that everything is not going to fall apart if you leave. This is even less likely to happen if you follow the second step and set up the proper procedures so your staff can run things when you are not there.

The third step is to put a manager in place to shift power away from a lot of people answering to you to just one person or a small handful of individuals who you trust will get things done. The fourth and final step is to get your tax situation in order. Depending on where you are from, where your business is incorporated and how long you will be traveling, it is possible to reduce your tax burden simply by living overseas.

For instance, US citizens living and earning money abroad can qualify for the Foreign Earned Income Exclusion and exempt their first $102,100 (in 2017) in income from taxes. This is true for any US person, including business owners, freelancers and anyone else who earns income while living overseas more than 330 days a year. For many, the mere savings in taxes alone is enough to pay for their travels or to take their business to the next level.[56]

One final tip is to bring an online element into your brick-and-mortar business. Andrew Henderson explains:

> Blogs, podcasts, and other online tools can be used as a cheap and targeted way to generate leads for a business that has no other ties to the online world. While I doubt my friend who is launching his own line of men's wallets would attract much interest to a podcast about wallets, he could certainly use a blog or podcast to establish himself as a fashion expert.[57]

While not everyone is going to sell wallets or begin a fashion podcast, you get the idea. If you want to be location independent, find a way to do what you are passionate about and the World Wide Web will be there to make it that much more profitable and possible – even when your business is bound to a set location.

Make Money From Your Home

One final tip for making money while you are on the road is to make money from renting your home. Depending on how long you are traveling, you can rent out your home long-term or increase your gains by posting your home on one of the short-term and vacation rental sites we discussed earlier, such as Airbnb.

Every family is different and will find a solution that works for them. Many families establish multiple sources of income, others make the sharing economy work in their favor, but they all make it happen one way or another. Here are some final perspectives from the families who have already found a way to finance their world schooling dreams:

Cliff Hsia

When you're abroad, you save on all kinds of different expenses that you wouldn't normally save at home. You can get creative about it. What we did for our gap year, we rented out our house and sold our car. We didn't get rid of everything we owned, but most of it, just because we wanted to unload and have a fresh start for when we came back. You can supplement your expenses at home. You don't have to give up everything, like sell your house. A lot of the stories are like that where it's all in or nothing. We weren't ready to sell everything. We wanted to take it in stages where we could actually come back to a life that we wanted.[40]

Jennifer Miller

Quit your job! It's difficult to give someone an outside-the-box education if you're living in an inside-the-box lifestyle. I understand that that's really hard for people and it's really scary when you're sitting on the other side of that divide. We've made two or three big leaps over the years in our careers and in our family structure and it's always terrifying...

You do it because it's the thing you're passionate about and you want to do it. If you can find a way to create an online income stream, the world really truly does become your oyster. You can stay home if you want to, if that's what you love, but you're not bound by that. And I think that figuring that out has been the single biggest tool that we have. We both work wherever we're at and that's what allows us to be wherever we want to be.[24]

Lainie Liberti

When we left, I shut my agency and I had savings and we sold almost everything that we owned so we had enough money to travel very comfortably. When we decided to make it an indefinite thing the second year after that, I did a little bit of freelance work based on my old career. I did some consulting and branding and some design work.

The third and fourth and fifth year, I was doing writing and selling ads on my website and that, at one point, was sustaining us. And the fifth, sixth and seventh year, Project World School has been sustaining us. So, a little bit of diversity, a little bit of this and a little bit of that. It hasn't just been one thing.

And, trust me, there have been probably fifteen times that we've been broke. Just trust that unfolding and allow everything to happen in a very fluid way and [don't go] into fear and all of that. Know that you always have a way.[29]

Brandon Pearce

The first step is to choose which approach/method appeals to you the most.... There are so many ways to finance your travels. There are as many ways to fund your travels as there are people. And there are so many different types of products and jobs and different things that you can create. It won't be starting a business for everyone. And it won't be finding a brand new job as a contractor for a company that wants you to work remotely, but it could be both for some people. You just have to tune in to yourself and figure out what appeals to you.[4]

Nancy Sathre-Vogel

Ultimately, it's going to be different for every person. All I can say, really, is to be creative, use your strengths and look at what you know. And don't only look at what you know in your professional life, but be willing and open to using your hobbies and other passions, because sometimes those things can be what leads to something that you could get paid for.

But it's so individual. Everybody comes in with their own unique set of skills and expertise and passions and interests; something that would work for me may not work for someone else at all. It's there, it's possible for all of us, but it won't necessarily be easy and it won't necessarily be your first try. As we try to branch out and do something we will fail, and if it's something that we are determined to do, we get up, brush ourselves off and try again with something else.[12]

Chapter Ten: The Game Plan

No one can deny the power of a good book. Every once in a while, some of us are lucky enough to come across a book that changes the way we see the world and what we want from the one life we have been given on this crazy planet. I became one of the lucky ones when, as an eleven-year-old girl, I came across "The True Confessions of Charlotte Doyle" by Avi.

The book tells the story of the daughter of an upper-class American family who, in 1832, is about to board the *Seahawk* and make the long voyage back to America after studying at a private girl's school in England. Despite warnings from the ship's crew that have scared away the other passengers, Charlotte's escort insists that she board the ship. The obedient, proper young lady ends up as the only passenger (and the only female) aboard the ship.

She eventually learns why the crew did not want passengers on the voyage as she discovers their plans for mutiny. The story follows Charlotte on her adventurous journey across the ocean as her cultured views are torn apart by the realities of the world outside her sheltered, sophisticated upbringing.

I read and reread that book. Every time, I would follow Charlotte through her journey as she insisted in the beginning to maintain her sophisticated dignity in the face of so many dirty, vile, mutinous sailors. Then, I would struggle with her as time, experience, and confrontation with stark reality began to change her views of the sailors she had once loathed and the captain she had clung to and respected.

I would then feel her exhilarating new freedom as she left behind her pretty dresses and "educated" (yet naive) notions and joined the mutinous sailors and became one herself. And I would always end the book with a burning desire to "be a pirate" too and live a life of true adventure traveling the seas.

Over time, "The True Confessions of Charlotte Doyle" changed the way I saw the world in two ways. First, it cemented in me a desire to pursue the unconventional and adventurous. Second, it gave me a healthy desire to question . . . everything! It made me look at my life, my culture, my religious beliefs, and my hopes and dreams for the future with a new, more critical perspective. I was determined to do as Charlotte did and see the world and myself with open eyes.

I wanted to know people for who they really were, not just the image the world expected me to believe. I wanted to gain the kind of knowledge that would allow me to have my own educated political beliefs. I wanted to know how much of what I wanted out of life was simply a result of my environment and culture; and I wanted to make sure that, in the end, my hopes and dreams were based on decisions I made for myself because I knew *why* they were important.

More than anything, I wanted to know if the beliefs I held closest to me were based on truth or if they were simply a product of my culture. In essence, I wanted to understand and make my life and beliefs my own.

After my third or fourth reading of the book, I was at the interesting age of 13 when boys were suddenly something other than those annoying kids on the playground I sometimes had to beat up. By thirteen I had experienced my own crush or two, but my little Charlotte heart had also recognized that middle-school love was a very superficial business (especially since I had recently faked a crush just to have something to talk about with my friends).

Now, with a fresh dose of "pirate perspective" from my most recent reading of the book, I was determined to conquer the superficiality of middle-school love and discover the world beyond teenage dreams of Prince Charming and magical prom nights.

One of the first things I locked onto in my inquiry of the culture of love was what seemed (to me, at the time) to be the typical life trajectory of the average small-town girl: grow up, get married, have babies. To a thirteen-year-old girl bound and determined to live an unconventional and adventurous life, this seemed to be the antithesis of all my dreams of adventure.

And so it was that at 13-years-old I came to the conclusion that I did *not* want to just grow up, get married, and have babies. I can still remember the moment I chose to confess my feelings on the matter to my mother. We were in the car – in between stores as we ran errands on a Saturday – and I decided that it was the best time to bring up the fact that I wanted to be a "pirate" and live a life of adventure . . . and I simply couldn't see how marriage and babies would ever allow me to achieve that.

I wanted the world to expect more from me than a pretty face, good cooking skills, and a perfectly organized home full of children and a successful husband. At the time, it seemed to be a hollow cultural expectation and I didn't fancy the idea of doing something so unadventurous simply due to cultural motives. I wanted to be a "pirate" and to explore the world and all my potential.

After hearing me out, my mother did something I will never forget. She did not say that I was being silly or that my view of motherhood was a bit immature; she didn't even tell me that I could live a little before I settled down. Instead, my mother began painting a beautiful picture of the life she had lived, including her adventures of swimming in the Red Sea, touring the Great Pyramids of Egypt, and dancing in the streets of Italy. All of these activities, she pointed out, she had done once she was already a mother.

Motherhood, in other words, would not equal an end to all my adventure.

In fact, my mother explained, even in comparison with these adventures, motherhood had been and forever would be her greatest adventure. I cannot put into words exactly how she said it all, but the power and commitment with which she spoke cut directly to my heart in such a way that I have never been able to forget that moment, nor her message.

My mother's story made a subtle, but very important, change to the way I approached my motherhood investigation. I was still very much an adventure-bound teenager with a determined desire to do more, see more, and change more in the world than what I judged (and forgive me for my adolescent prejudices) to be the aspirations of the average boy-crazy, motherhood-anticipating female. However, I was beginning to understand the importance of motherhood and family in an entirely new light.

My mother's claim that motherhood in and of itself was an adventure had piqued my interest. Her story made me stop and ask myself *why* motherhood was so important. I was reminded that Charlotte Doyle had been able to achieve an adventurous life, not because she initially sought adventure, but because she had sought the truth. Truth gave her adventure, and suddenly I wanted the full truth about what it meant to be a woman and a mother.

What I found was undeniable evidence for the case my mother had made about the invaluable role of mothers and family. While my worth as an individual was not determined by my ability to marry and have children, that in no way ruled out the importance of motherhood and family. In fact, what I found over years of investigation brought about an entirely new perspective.

During my high school and college years, my long-held desire to have a positive impact in the world and to help create strong societies led me to study poverty, development, politics, economics, history, education and even a second language. In those studies, and even through my travels, I found that family is at the heart of it all. Families – in all their different shapes and sizes – are key to the success of humanity.

This newfound understanding did nothing to curb my quest for an unconventionally adventurous life, though. I clung to my mother's story of travel and adventure even after she had children like a lifeline. There had to be a way to be a good mother and a great adventurer at the same time.

It was in Mexico – while conducting research on rural student dropout rates – that I met my husband and a completely new adventure began. My husband and I chose to live in Mexico after we were married and, together, we have experienced a more daring and exciting life than I could have possibly imagined as a 13-year-old girl dreaming of adventure on the high sea. Growing up and getting married turned out to be a bigger adventure than all of my wildest dreams.

And then I became a mother. Of all the things I have ever done, being a mom has been the most physically, mentally, emotionally, and spiritually demanding thing I have ever done. It is an adventure words fail to describe and that a lifetime of adventure-seeking would never find. There is nothing like hearing my baby's heartbeat for the first time or seeing his little body on the ultrasound screen. There is nothing like watching my little boy learn and grow and discover new things, new abilities and new adventures of his own. Nothing touches it.

And now I want to ensure that this little ball of curiosity grows to become a good person, a happy person, a person who loves the world and the people in it, and a person who is capable of contributing to the progress of all that is good. Because of that, I look at world schooling not just as a form of adventure for myself and my family but as a means of fulfilling the solemn responsibility I have as a mother to teach my children.

I share this story for a couple reasons. First, because there are many world travelers out there who may worry that family will keep them from traveling the world and, because of this belief, choose not to have children or postpone doing so because they are not ready to settle down. I am here to tell you that you do not have to choose between one or the other. If you want a family, you can choose family. If you want to travel, you can choose travel. And if you want both, you can choose both.

The second reason I share my story is to illustrate how important it is for each of us to truly understand our motives and responsibilities as world schooling parents. We can have both family and adventure, but we must also understand the responsibilities that come with combining the two.

Creating a successful game plan to revolutionize our children's education through world travel requires a deeper understanding of our basic purpose in doing so. We owe it to ourselves and to our children to understand what it is we really want from the experience – not just what we want the experience to be like, but why we want the experience in the first place. Brandon Pearce explained,

> Making a lifestyle change like this, even if it brings you everything that you're dreaming, isn't necessarily going to make you happy. Happiness is not an external thing, it's a choice that we make in each moment regardless of our circumstances. It's a habit and we have to cultivate it every step.

> I've had moments where I've had everything – plenty of money in the bank, I'm living in this gorgeous villa with a cook and housekeeper and driver and nanny and we've got this beautiful pool and a view and everything is just perfect – but something happens and I'm grumpy and mad and angry that day and I'm not enjoying my life. It's not about the external circumstances, it's about how we're looking at things and how we're choosing to live and how we're choosing to think and feel and direct our energies.[4]

Knowing the purpose behind your travels will provide you with the big picture that can sometimes get lost in the rush of bumpy bus rides and tough days. That is why defining the purpose behind your world schooling adventures is the foundation for all the other steps that follow in arming your world schooling game plan.

Step One: Define Your Educational Philosophy

Once you know why you want the adventure of world schooling, the first step to making that dream a reality is to define your educational philosophy. Your reasons behind that philosophy will affect much of how you choose to educate your children and, consequently, affect everyone else in your family. Feel free to involve your children in the process to get their perspectives too. You will be much more successful if you take them into account from the beginning.

Read and research about the various methods that are already being used. Besides the books listed in Chapter Eight, a good place to start is with the Home Life Academy where you can read a quick summary of each method and take two different quizzes, 1) to better understand what kind of homeschool philosophy you follow and 2) the ways by which your children best learn (visual, auditory, verbal or kinesthetic).

You will likely need a period of trial and error to figure out what works best for you, your children, and your life situation. Be flexible and adaptable. Allow choice. You may feel strongly about one educational philosophy, but if it is not working for one of your children, be flexible enough to find what will work for them. Empower them with the same knowledge that you have gained that their life is theirs to design and choose.

Of course, they are your children and will need your parental guidance, but help them take responsibility for their own learning — even if it is not something you would choose for them. People respond much better when they are offered the freedom to choose for themselves.

Every child is different and even the same child will progress and change over time. Successful world schooling requires flexibility. Kathryn, a world schooling mother said this of her family's world schooling educational "game plan":

I don't unschool or follow a structured approach. But sometimes I do both. Sometimes the children want to be really structured, other times they just want to learn as they go. I guess you could call it eclectic? I call it life and going with the flow.

However, I do want some engagement and so when I feel that they're just flatly refusing to do anything at all I change my approach.

Just as I don't want to feel penned in by a school or even a house at times, I also wouldn't want to feel as if an educational philosophy of any kind was restricting me to only one way of learning.

Different people, different families, different children within one family, all learn, grow, develop differently. The huge advantage of any type of educational style outside of school is that it can be developed to meet individual needs.[58]

Finally, when it comes to choosing your educational philosophy, avoid getting caught up in what everyone else is doing. Recognize that other people take different approaches because they have different children, different strengths and weaknesses and different life and travel situations. Avoid comparing. Do what works for you. As Jennifer Miller said:

Read less about what everybody else is doing and invest more time in your own kids and in your own family. People get so bound up in the "would of, could of, should of" and the debates between factions. There are people who are passionately sure that they are right and other people are wrong and people get caught in this net of trying to do it the way that other people would like to do it. Or, they'll look at someone's kids who are downstream from theirs by maybe four or five years and think, "Wow, I want my kids to be just like that so let's do that." That's a terrible way to parent or to educate! The more you can just invest in your own family and trial and error, the happier you will be at it at any rate.[24]

Figure out what you believe, how you want to educate, be flexible and open to changing in the face of your children's needs and interests, and avoid comparing what works for you to what everyone else is doing.

Step Two: Pick a World Schooling Strategy

Depending on your educational philosophy, you will likely find one world schooling strategy more appealing than another. Your life situation and travel preferences will also affect what world schooling strategy you choose to stick with.

Not all families, for instance, like to travel on a permanent basis and will choose to be Settled Globetrotters who travel on occasion and return to their home base after each trip. Other families may value language immersion to such a degree that they will choose to follow the Unconventional Traditionalist path and enroll their children in local schools wherever they go.

Parents who believe that children need some parental guidance and prefer a more systematic approach may fit somewhere between Structured Adventurers and Settled Globetrotters, depending on their travel preferences. And unschoolers will likely embrace the World un-Schoolers strategy. Many will pick and choose between the different strategies for a more eclectic approach, which is a perfectly valid option as well.

Your travel preferences can also impact your world schooling approach beyond your educational philosophies. Cliff Hsia laid out some great advice and questions world schooling hopefuls should ask themselves to better understand what kind of world schooling strategy and travel lifestyle will work best for them:

> First of all, you've got to figure out what your comfort level is. How long? How much do you want to spend? Where do you want to go? What kind of environments do you want to be in? Do you want to be in metropolitan cities or rural areas? You have to be self-aware of what your comfort levels are and map your experiences around those. You also have to be aware of your kids' level of comfort.

For example, going to Nicaragua as our first country, we probably wouldn't go back to that type of country again. I probably would because I like those types of environments, but I discovered that my wife is not a big fan of really developing countries. That was tough on her. We found our sweet spot going to different big cities and having the resources there. We would be able to find anything we needed, we had schools nearby and public transportation and what not. So that's the model we went with.

For other parents, when you first get started you might not know what your comfort level is, so just take it in small steps. You don't have to commit to upping everything and taking your kids to wherever and go to all these different countries and put them in all these different schools around the world.

My advice would be to take it just one step at a time and take it in small steps in the beginning. Start with a small trip – maybe nearby or to another English speaking country or a European country that's more modernized – and then move on from there and see if you're more adventurous and want to do a longer trip like one month or two months and see if, maybe similar to us, you want to put your kids into school there. See how that works out and see if you're ready to move all-in and do longer types of trips like a gap year where you can put your kids in school for six months in Spain or something like that and then travel all around Europe.

There are so many options and it can seem kind of overwhelming in the beginning trying to create these experiences, but we just took one trip at a time and slowly and in small increments. It just worked its way up to where we had enough courage and motivation and we were financially secure with enough savings to take that big leap of faith and just go all in for a gap year.

And some people might go even further than that. They might become expats and just move abroad after those types of experiences. There's really a whole spectrum of experiences that you can provide for your children with world schooling. It's really just finding what's the right mix for your family.[40]

Step Three: Embrace the Opportunity

The next step in formulating your world schooling game plan is to embrace the abundance of opportunities out there to make it all possible. We have discussed at length the educational and financial resources that are available to those who want to take advantage of them. Now, it is just a matter of figuring out which ones fit with your philosophies and strategies and then embracing those opportunities 100%.

The educational material that was once only available to scholars is now freely available to the world at large. Do not waste that opportunity! Technology has given us a once-in-a-millennium chance to revolutionize the way we educate our children. You do not have to stick to the path that society has been following for hundreds of years. Embrace the change and take your place at the front lines of the education revolution!

But don't stop there. Embrace the opportunities of the digital era to not only fund your family's travel lifestyle but also to sustain your family long-term. As Taylor Pearson put it:

[The] same tools, the means of production, available exclusively to the wealthy for all of human history, are now in your hands. Multimillion-dollar businesses are run using a laptop, Skype, and an internet connection. That is the world in which we live. One where the future is not defined. One where it's up to each individual, group, and society to write the future for themselves.... Never before has a generation held the pen to write their future in the way we do– but it will not write itself (p.260).[17]

Put behind you the linear thinking that has locked you into a set schedule of superfluous responsibilities and a life trajectory that is impossible to change. Follow your passions. Create value and you will find that you will be rewarded warmly for it. There is a reason you crave freedom and self-determination, embrace those feelings and design the life *you* want. It is not just a dream for some far distant future when you have finished "working for the man" and raising your family decades from now. This is a life that you can leverage to sustain and raise your family in one of the most extraordinary ways possible.

Embrace that truth and then choose it. Once you do, all that's left is step four...

Step Four: Go For It!

Once you know what you want, do not wait around worrying in fear that things will not work out. Just go for it! The night before my flight left for Mexico, my brother found me close to tears, hiding under the covers of my bed. I had traveled many times before, but for some reason I was terrified of Mexico. I had heard horror stories pretty much all of my life about the country south of the border and I was almost certain that the moment I got off the plane, someone was going to rob me.

But I went for it. I got on that plane. Five years later, I am married to the love of my life (from Mexico) with a beautiful little boy, living the life of adventure I had dreamed of since I was young, and all thanks to Mexico. Have I been robbed? Oh yes! But I learned that life goes on, even after your material possessions are taken from you.

Instead of focusing on the fear of all that could go wrong, think about all of the good that will not come into your life if you do not go for your dreams. In the end, we are really robbing ourselves of the experiences that we can have if we live in fear of the 'what ifs.' I have found that even when the 'what ifs' happen, they were more than worth the reward.

So, go for it! This book is full of resources that could have you overplanning and keeping you from ever actually acting. Plan, budget, figure out what you want from the experience, but allow room for spontaneity, down days, new curiosities and lots of unexpected adventures. Give yourself time to enjoy every location and avoid the rush of the typical tourist trying to see every site in a matter of days before they have to head back to the office. You have time to see the world how you want to see it. Do not forget that.

Finally, the key to making the leap and going for it all comes down to trust. Trust that things will work out. Trust – despite criticism from friends and family and even strangers – that your kids are learning. Trust that it is happening, even if you cannot see it. Trust that taking your kids out into the world will provide them with an education more powerful than anything they could ever get inside a classroom. Trust that you have the talents, knowledge and abilities necessary to facilitate your child's learning and a world schooling lifestyle. Trust yourself. Trust them. And trust the experience.

Then go for it. If we can live without fear and show our children how to live the life of their choosing, we will be doing more for them than we could possibly imagine. World schooling is so much more than travel and education. It is so much more than a lifestyle of the rich. World schooling is a movement of parents who know the possibilities and embrace them.

As we do, we can change the world one child at a time. Come and join the revolution!

Notes

[1] Menken, A., Ashman, H., & O'Hara, P. (1991). Belle (Reprise). Hollywood: Disney. Retrieved from https://itunes.apple.com/us/album/ beauty-and-the-beast-soundtrack-from-the-motion-picture/id390433307

[2] Seth Godin. (2012). STOP STEALING DREAMS: On the future of education & what we can do about it.. Retrieved from https://www. youtube.com/watch?v=sXpbONjV1Jc

[3] Gray, P. (2013). Free to Learn: Why Unleashing the Instinct to Play Will Make Our Children Happier, More Self-Reliant, and Better Students for Life (1st ed.). United States of America: Basic Books. https://www.amazon.com/Free-Learn-Unleashing-Instinct-Self-Reliant/dp/0465025994

[4] Pearce, Brandon. Wednesday, November 9, 2016. Private interview. PearceOnEarth.

[5] Prince, Daniel. Wednesday, November 9, 2016. Private interview. Princes Off the Grid.

[6] Hewitt, B. (2014). Home Grown: Adventures in Parenting off the Beaten Path, Unschooling, and Reconnecting with the Natural World (1st ed.). Boston, Massachusetts: Roost Books. https://www.amazon.com/Home-Grown-Adventures-Unschooling-Reconnecting/dp/ 1611801699

[7] John Dewey, "Individual Psychology and Education," The Philosopher, 12, 1934 http://www.ascd.org/ASCD/pdf/journals/ed_update/eu201207_infographic.pdf

[8] Singer, A. (2016). What Is the Purpose of Education?. The Huffington Post. Retrieved 10 March 2017, from http://www.huffing tonpost.com/alan-singer/what-is-the-purpose-of-ed_b_9185702.html

[9] Roosevelt, E. (1930). Good Citizenship: The Purpose of Education. Pictorial Review, (31). Retrieved from https://www2.gwu.edu/~erpapers/documents/articles/goodcitizenship.cfm

[10] Khan, S. (2012). The One World Schoolhouse: Education Reimagined (1st ed.). United States: Grand Central Publishing. https://www.amazon.com/One-World-Schoolhouse-Education-Reimagined/dp/1455508373

[11] Orr, D. (1991). What Is Education For?. Context Institute. Retrieved 10 March 2017, from http://www.context.org/iclib/ic27/orr/

[12] Sathre-Vogel, Nancy. Tuesday, November 15, 2016. Private interview. Family on Bikes.

[13] Camera, L. (2016). High School Seniors Aren't College-Ready. U.S. News. Retrieved from http://www.usnews.com/news/articles/2016-04-27/high-school-seniors-arent-college-ready-naep-data-show

[14] Ward, A. (2012). It's a stitch up! How seven out of 10 young people don't know how to sew a button. Mail Online. Retrieved 11 March 2017, from http://www.dailymail.co.uk/news/article-2213723/ Young-adults-useless-basic-tasks.html#ixzz4UMLSouL3

[15] Bennett, J. (2014). Majority of Teens Say They Don't Know How to Change a Tire. WSJ. Retrieved 11 March 2017, from http://www.wsj.com/articles/majority-of-teens-say-they-dont-know-how-to-change-a-tire-1409025661

[16] Branagh, E. (2011). University freshers lack life skills, says survey. The Independent. Retrieved 11 March 2017, from http://www.independent.co.uk/news/uk/home-news/university-freshers-lack-life-skills-says-survey-2361129.html

[17] Pearson, T. (2015). The End of Jobs: Money, Meaning and Freedom Without the 9-to-5 (1st ed.). https://www.amazon.com/End-Jobs-Meaning-9-5-ebook/dp/B010L8SYRG

[18] Smith, C. (2015). The Changing World of Work 4: The "Signal" Value of Credentials Is Eroding. Of Two Minds. Retrieved from http://www.oftwominds.com/blogapr15/signal-erosion4-15.html

[19] Scott Curwood, J. What Happened to Kindergarten? | Scholastic. Beta.scholastic.com. Retrieved 11 March 2017, from https://beta.scholastic.com/teachers/articles/teaching-content/what-happened-kindergarten/

[20] Sathre-Vogel, N. (2014). Roadschooling: The Ultimate Guide to Education Through Travel (1st ed.). United States: Old Stone Publishing. https://www.amazon.com/Roadschooling-Ultimate-Education-Through-Travel/dp/0983718741

[21] Hilgevoord, J. & Uffink, J. (2017). The Uncertainty Principle. Plato.stanford.edu. Retrieved 11 March 2017, from https://plato.stanford.edu/entries/qt-uncertainty/ (Heisenberg 1927: 174–5)

[22] MacDonald, F. (2015). No More Physics and Maths, Finland to Stop Teaching Individual Subjects. ScienceAlert. Retrieved 11 March 2017, from http://www.sciencealert.com/no-more-physics-and-maths-finland-to-stop-teaching-individual-subjects

[23] Strauss, V. (2015, February 12). What's the purpose of education in the 21st century? The Washington Post. Retrieved March 10, 2017, from https://www.washingtonpost.com/news/answer-sheet/wp/ 2015/02/12/whats-the-purpose-of-education-in-the-21st-century/

[24] Miller, Jennifer. Friday, November 11, 2016. Private interview. Edventure Project.

[25] Gillett, R. (2015, July 23). Research says this is what you need to teach your kids in kindergarten if you ever want them to go to college or get a job. Retrieved March 11, 2017, from http://www.businessinsider.com /future-success-could-be-determined-early-2015-7#ixzz3hCRlz0Oc

[26] Miller, J. (2013, March 8). Homeschooling on the Road: How to Roadschool. Retrieved March 11, 2017, from https://wandrlymagazine.com/article/roadschooling-101/

[27] Frost, M. (2009). The new global student: skip the SAT, save thousands on tuition, and get a truly international education. New York: Three Rivers Press. doi:https://www.amazon.com/New-Global-Student-Thousands-International/dp/0307450627

[28] Robinson, K. (2007, January 06). Do schools kill creativity? Retrieved March 11, 2017, from https://www.youtube.com/watch?v=iG9CE55wbtY

[29] Liberti, Lainie. Thursday, December 8, 2016. Private interview. Raising Miro.

[30] Robinson, K. (2010, May 24). Bring on the learning revolution. Retrieved March 11, 2017, from https://www.youtube.com/watch?v=kFMZrEABdw4

[31] Homeschooling - Class Dismissed Movie - Official Trailer. (2012, October 30). Retrieved March 11, 2017, from https://youtu.be/0FMrQXkFCxA

[32] Isenberg, E. J. (2007). What Have We Learned About Homeschooling? Peabody Journal of Education, 82(2-3), 387-409. doi:10.1080/01619560701312996 http://www.tandfonline.com/doi/citedby/10.1080/016195607013129 96?scroll=top&needAccess=true

[33] Martin-Chang S, Gould ON, and Meuse, R E. The impact of schooling on academic achievement: Evidence from homeschooled and traditionally schooled students. Canadian Journal of Behavioural Science 43(3): 195-202. - See more at: http://www.parentingscience.com/homeschoolingoutcomes.html#sth ash.n7vKjsZT.dpuf

[34] Gerzon, Eli. Worldschooling. (n.d.). Retrieved March 11, 2017, from http://www.eligerzon.com/worldschooling.php

[35] Homeschool Group Hug. (2017, February 18). What is Deschooling? Retrieved March 11, 2017, from http://homeschoolgrouphug.com/what-is-deschooling/

[36] Griffith, M. (1998). The unschooling handbook: how to use the whole world as your child's classroom. New York: Three Rivers Press. doi:https://www.amazon.com/Unschooling-Handbook-Whole-Childs-Classroom/dp/0761512764

[37] Martin, J. C. (2016). Give your child the world: raising globally minded kids one book at a time. Grand Rapids, MI: Zondervan. https://www.amazon.com/Give-Your-Child-World-Globally/dp/0310344131

[38] Miller, J. (2015, June 22). Educational Travel: How to Get Permission and Justify the Experience to Your Local School. Retrieved March 11, 2017, from http://www.bootsnall.com/articles/12-08/educational-travel-how-to-take-your-kids-out-of-school.html

[39] Hsia, C. (2015, September 1). Why We World School Our Children. Retrieved March 11, 2017, from http://www.livefamilytravel.com/why-we-world-school-our-children/

[40] Hsia, Cliff. Thursday, November 10, 2016. Private interview. Live Family Travel.

[41] Sutcliffe, T. (2013, May 28). Why We Won't Continue the Chinese School Experiment. Retrieved March 11, 2017, from http://www.escapeartistes.com/2013/05/28/why-we-wont-continue-the-chinese-school-experiment/

[42] Sutcliffe, T. (2015, September 14). How Does High School Work After Homeschooling While Travelling? Retrieved March 11, 2017, from http://www.escapeartistes.com/2015/04/07/how-does-high-school-work-after-homeschooling-while-travelling/

[43] Comment from Ariel Gibson in the Facebook Group Worldschoolers. Permission to use her comment granted January 26, 2017.

[44] Oxenreider, T. (2015, January 23). Tsh's worldschool day in the life (with a 4-, 7-, and 9-year-old). Retrieved March 11, 2017, from http:// simplehomeschool.net/worldschool/

[45] Liberti, L. (2017, March 08). About. Retrieved March 11, 2017, from http://www.raisingmiro.com/about/

[46] Sztupovszky, A. (2016, August 26). 10 Things I've Learned As An Unschooling Parent. Retrieved March 11, 2017, from http://world schooladventures.com/2016/08/26/10-things-ive-learned-as-an-unschooling-parent/

[47] Comment from Emily Horos in the Facebook Group Worldschoolers. Permission to use her comment granted February 15, 2017.

[48] Aitkenread, L. (2016, December 22). World Schooling is a Wild Ride That Just Might Be the Best Thing For Your Kids. Retrieved March 11, 2017, from http://www.parent.co/world-schooling-is-the-new-home-schooling/

[49] Khan Academy. (n.d.). Retrieved March 11, 2017, from https://www. khanacademy.org/partner-content/pixar

[50] World Schooling Book Interview [E-mail to the author, from Lainie Liberti]. (2016, December 8). Permission given to use, edit and change for the purposes of the book World Schooling.

[51] Miller, H. (2016, September 10). 10 Ways World-schooling Has Ruined My Childhood. Retrieved March 11, 2017, from http://www. edventuregirl.com/10-ways-world-schooling-has-ruined-my-childhood/

[52] O'Donnell, S. (n.d.). Resources for Traveling Homeschoolers. Retrieved March 11, 2017, from http://alittleadrift.com/homeschooling/

[53] Sztupovszky, A. (January 8). How We Fund Long-Term Family Travel. Retrieved March 11, 2017, from http://worldschooladventures.com/2017/01/08/how-we-fund-long-term-family-travel/

[54] For more great ideas on finances for family travelers, check out this article http://www.vagabondfamily.org/blog/finance/travel-budgeting-tips-help-for-planning-and-on-the-road/ and http://www.vagabondfamily.org/blog/finance/why-a-travel-budget-is-different-from-a-household-budget-and-why-it-even-matters/

[55] Pearce, B. (2016, August 18). Income On The Go – 7 Ways To Fund A Travel Lifestyle. Retrieved March 11, 2017, from http://pearceonearth.com /income-on-the-go-7-ways-to-fund-a-travel-lifestyle/

[56] Henderson, A. (2016, November 15). Four steps to make ANY business location independent. Retrieved March 11, 2017, from http://nomad capitalist.com/2016/11/21/steps-make-business-location-independent/

[57] Henderson, A. (2016, January 20). How to make any business a location independent business. Retrieved March 11, 2017, from http://nomad capitalist.com/2015/07/24/how-to-make-any-business-location-independent/

[58] Comment from Kathryn in the Facebook Group Worldschoolers. Permission to use her comment granted February 2017.

[59] Dee, T. S., & Sievertsen, H. H. (october 2015). The Gift of Time? School Starting Age and Mental Health. *National Bureau of Economic Research,* working paper series. doi:10.3386/w21610

[60] Miller, R. (n.d.). A Map of the Alternative Education Landscape. Retrieved March 19, 2017, from http://www.educationrevolution.org/store/resources/alternatives/mapoflandscape/

Made in the USA
Monee, IL
01 April 2021

64373778R00111